Fortress • 3

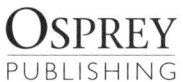

OSPREY
PUBLISHING

# U-Boat Bases and Bunkers 1941–45

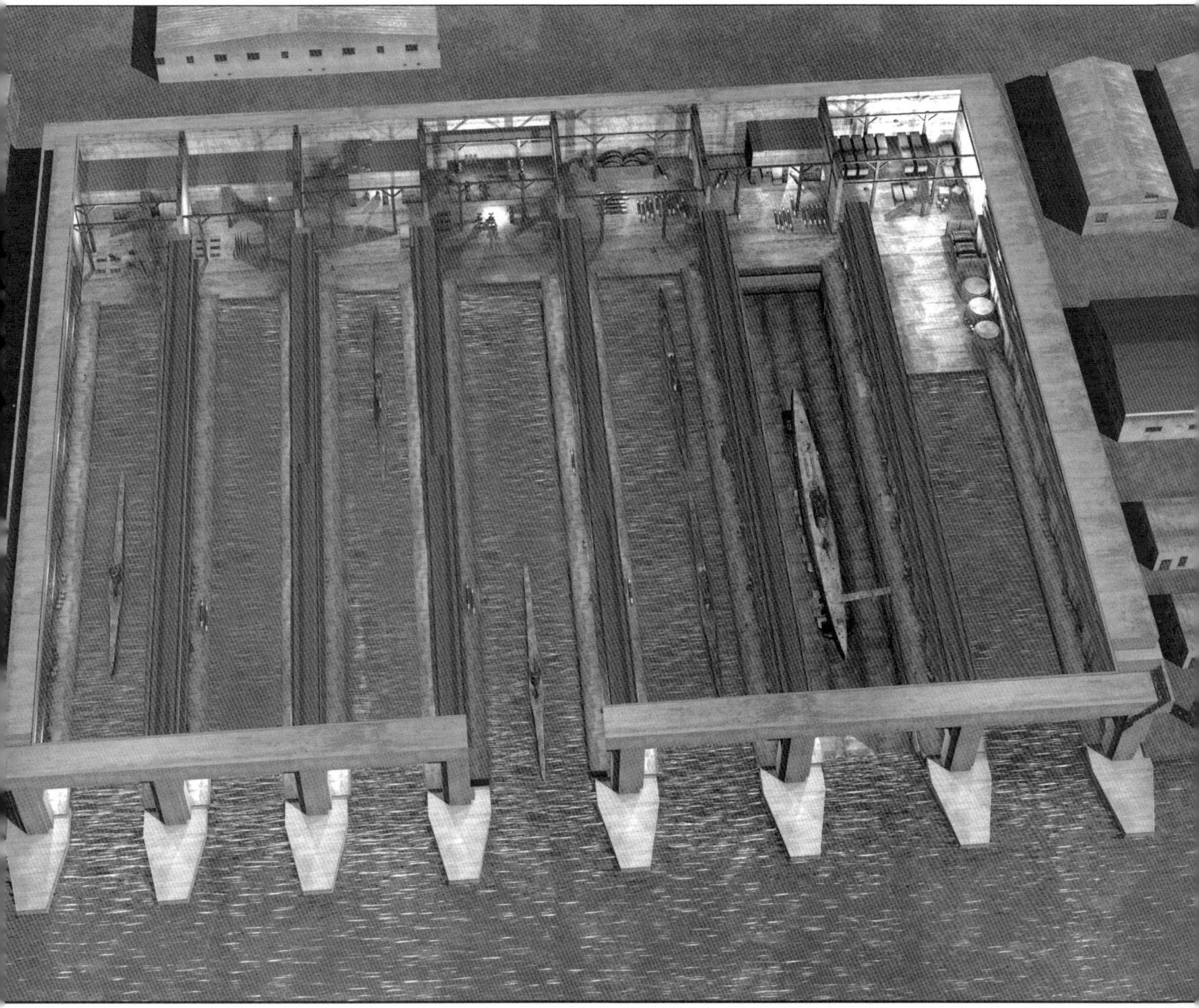

Gordon Williamson • Illustrated by Ian Palmer
Series editors Marcus Cowper and Nikolai Bogdanovic

First published in Great Britain in 2003 by Osprey Publishing,
Midland House, West Way, Botley, Oxford OX2 0PH, United Kingdom.
443 Park Avenue South, New York, NY 10016, USA
Email: info@ospreypublishing.com
© 2003 Osprey Publishing Ltd.

ISBN 1 84176 556 2

Editorial: Ilios Publishing, Oxford, UK (www.iliospublishing.com)
Design: Ken Vail Graphic Design, Cambridge, UK
Index by Alison Worthington
Originated by The Electronic Page Company, Cwmbran, UK
Printed and bound in China by L-Rex Printing Company Ltd

05 06 07 08 09   10 9 8 7 6 5 4 3

CIP data for this publication is available from the British Library

FOR A CATALOGUE OF ALL BOOKS PUBLISHED BY OSPREY MILITARY
AND AVIATION PLEASE CONTACT:

NORTH AMERICA
Osprey Direct, 2427 Bond Street, University Park, IL 60466, USA
E-mail: info@ospreydirectusa.com

ALL OTHER REGIONS
Osprey Direct UK, P.O. Box 140, Wellingborough,
Northants, NN8 2FA, UK
E-mail: info@ospreydirect.co.uk

www.ospreypublishing.com

# Acknowledgements

First and foremost, I would like to express my gratitude to
Horst Bredow, director of the U-Boot Archiv for supplying most
of the photographic material in this work and for making the
facilities of the Archiv available for research. I would also like
to thank him for the warm welcome and encouragement that
awaited me in Cuxhaven. Kevin Matthews also made the selection
of photographic material infinitely easier by lending his sterling
assistance in wading through the vast photographic archive
material in Cuxhaven. I would also like to thank Chris Boonzaier
of Germany and Hans Lauritzen of Norway for helping to source
photographs of some of the bunkers as they are today.

## Conversion table

1 cm = 0.3937 in.
1 m = 1.0936 yd
1 km = 0.6214 mile
1 kg = 2.2046 lb
1 tonne = 0.9842 ton (UK)

# Contents

# Introduction

The German U-Boat fleet, under the command of Konteradmiral (later Grossadmiral and Commander-in-Chief Navy) Karl Dönitz, had shown its potential almost from the very outbreak of war. In September 1939, an early Type VIIb vessel under the command of Kapitänleutnant Gunther Prien succeeded in penetrating the Royal Navy's Home Fleet anchorage at Scapa Flow, believed to be virtually impregnable, and sank the battleship *Royal Oak*. To compound Britain's agony, *U-47* then escaped with relative ease.

At this point in time, however, U-Boats still faced a tricky and lengthy voyage through German waters into the North Sea, or through the English Channel and on to the Atlantic, which served to reduce their operational service period and increase their vulnerability to enemy attack. Despite their deadly effectiveness, U-Boats were of course much more susceptible to damage than surface craft. If caught on the surface their pressure hulls could easily be damaged, rendering them incapable of diving. They would then be virtually helpless.

Prior to the outbreak of war, U-Boats were often to be seen moored alongside their designated flotilla tender or 'mother ship'. The clear danger posed by enemy air attack against them (even though Royal Air Force raids against German targets were initially rather ineffective) saw plans drawn up for protective concrete bunkers in German naval bases such as Helgoland, Hamburg and Kiel.

Following the fall of first Norway and then France and the Low Countries in the summer of 1940, a large number of additional operational bases became available to the U-Boot Waffe, and these were put to use almost immediately. In some cases, the Germans were simply re-occupying bases they had already made use of during World War I. The first such bases had been established in the Belgian port of Bruges in August 1917. These had proven highly successful, with the U-Boat pens remaining largely undamaged despite numerous British bombing raids.

Grossadmiral Raeder, C-in-C of the German Navy, during a visit to the Lorient base. In the background can be seen a Type IX U-Boat which, having been winched up from the docking pen, now sits on its special cradle on the traversing unit.

With the Norwegian and Channel ports under their control, the German navy now had easy access to the North Sea and the Atlantic. This allowed them a faster turnaround time on operations and thus increased the number of boats at sea at any one time. Dönitz worked on a simple three-way split of his available submarines, with one third in transit to or from operations, one third on combat patrol, and the remaining third in port being fitted out, resupplied or overhauled.

U-Boat bases were quickly established at Bergen and Trondheim in Norway, and at Brest, Lorient, St Nazaire, La Pallice and Bordeaux in France. Although these new bases had considerable advantages for Dönitz, they also brought his U-Boats within much easier reach of the RAF.

Concrete bunkers had proven their effectiveness at Bruges during World War I: in the spring of 1941 the Germans capitalised on their previous experience in this area and built new bunkers along very similar lines at all of the main U-Boat bases in France and Norway. These huge concrete edifices were erected in Germany too, at Helgoland, Kiel and Hamburg. Operational bases were not the only ones to be provided with these gigantic shelters: near Bremen, an entire U-Boat construction plant for the advanced Type XXI boats was built within a massive concrete bunker on the banks of the River Weser.

Initially, these bunkers were considered virtually bombproof. As the war progressed, however, the RAF developed heavier and heavier bombs, and in 1943 many of the bunkers were provided with extensive strengthening to their roofs, as well as heavy anti-aircraft defences. Some of the roofs of these bunkers were now over 7m thick. Additional roofing was added to some bunkers, spaced some way above the main roof.

The two-pen Scorff bunker at Lorient in the final stages of construction, watched over by an army guard. The raised central structure on the roof housed a flak gun for defence against low-flying enemy aircraft.

LEFT **Long-range defences of the French bases**
Faced with the threat of intensive Allied bombing raids, the first significant bunker defensive measure which would come into play was the Luftwaffe's system of early-warning radar and spotter posts. At various sites along the French coast were establishments equipped with the Freya and Würzburg radar systems (**1** and **2**). These would detect formations of Allied bombers approaching the coast. Depending on the time of day, single-engined day fighters (such as the Fw 190, **3**) or twin-engined Me 110 or Ju 88 night-fighters would be scrambled to intercept the enemy. Allied bombers could boast fairly powerful defensive weaponry, particularly when flying in close formation, but despite this many fell victim to the determined attacks of the Luftwaffe fighters. Those who survived such attacks would face a concentrated barrage of heavy anti-aircraft fire from large-calibre weapons (such as the 12.8cm flak gun, **4**) which protected

important installations such as the ports in occupied France.

In many cases poor visibility, bad weather or heavy cloud over the target prevented a number of planes from reaching their objective, as shown by events at Brest. On 3 September 1941, from a total of 140 RAF bombers which set out to attack the base only 53 actually made it to their target, the remainder having to return home. In another fairly typical raid, on 18 December 1941, 47 bombers left bases in England to attack the bunker. Six of these were shot down. Although two bombs landed in the water near the bunker (causing a pressure wave which killed five people inside because the pen doors were open), only five bombs landed on or near the bunker: these caused no significant damage to the structure. At the end of the day, the single greatest factor in the successful defence of the bunker was its inherent, massive strength (**5**).

Even the much vaunted bunker-busting 'Tallboy' bombs, weighing over five tons each and carrying over two tons of high explosive, usually failed to have much effect on the reinforced bunkers – though these vain attempts to put them out of action totally devastated the cities in which these bases were established.

In fact, these constructions were so strong that most of them survived the war almost unscathed. In some cases, attempts were made to demolish parts of them, but the effort required was so huge that most were left as they were. Almost all of the bunkers described in this work still exist, and many are still used as naval establishments. Both the Norwegian and French navies use some of the bunker facilities in their respective ports and the German Bundesmarine still uses part of the gigantic Valentin factory bunker at Bremen as a storage facility. Many of the bunkers still show clear traces of the original disruptive-pattern camouflage paint schemes, patriotic slogans, and warning notices painted on their walls.

A good number of them are now in private hands, generally used as storage facilities and many may still be visited. In some cases, such as the Fink II bunker in Hamburg, the entrances were simply dynamited to prevent members of the public gaining access and the bunkers abandoned, still with U-Boats inside.

In 1987, the past was brought back to life when a German Type VIIc U-Boat sailed once again from the bunker at La Pallice. The boat was a replica specially made for the successful submarine movie *Das Boot*.

Given the difficulty of dismantling or destroying these massive structures, it seems likely that those that have survived thus far will be with us for some time to come.

This interior view shows one of the highly important dry-dock-capable pens in which a Type IX is undergoing a major overhaul and repairs. The depth of the pen itself is clear to see. Note also the exterior doors in the background, and the gap between the top of these doors and the roof of the pen. Also note the powerful arc lights along the pen wall which allowed work to continue around the clock if necessary.

# Design and development

The U-Boat bunkers were but one aspect of Germany's programme of defensive construction. Similar protective housing was planned to shelter S-Boote (E-Boats) and Räum-Boote (R-Boats) and to provide protected locks: damage to these could effectively seal off a port. In addition storage bunkers for munitions and *matériel*, general defensive pillboxes and artillery bunkers were planned. It should also be remembered that the work on the U-Boat bunkers effectively competed for materials and manpower with the construction of the Atlantic Wall coastal defences.

## Construction

As far as the German navy was concerned, the responsibility for providing these defensive structures belonged to the Naval Construction Department (Marinebauwesens) under the command of Ministerialdirektor Eckhardt. The experience of building similar large-scale defensive structures on the German naval base at Helgoland was put to good use when the U-Boat bases began to appear in the various captured French ports in 1941, and the general designs themselves closely followed the basic principles established during the construction of the Imperial German Navy U-Boat base at Bruges.

Actual construction of the U-Boat bunkers fell to the Organisation Todt (OT), the state construction agency under the control of Dr Fritz Todt. Todt had been given the task of completing Germany's West Wall defences in 1938, and to do so had assembled a virtual army of construction workers. It is estimated that well over 300,000 men were drafted into the organisation, living in camps erected by the building firms which had been awarded the construction contracts. The Organisation Todt employed thousands of German technical specialists and tradesmen to oversee this army of labourers. After the outbreak of war, some of these workers were legitimately recruited from abroad, but others were little

The Bordeaux U-Boat pens under construction. This aerial view shows the sheer size of the construction site. The basic layout is already clearly visible with the individual pen foundations completed and the separating walls between the pens being erected. To the rear of the pens can be seen the structures which would contain the various workshop areas. No site this large can be hidden from enemy aerial reconnaissance, yet the U-Boat bunker complexes were all successfully completed without incurring significant damage from enemy attacks.

The bunker complex at Brest in the final stages of construction. The two pens at far right are still being worked on and are protected by cofferdams. Water that has entered the pens is being discharged by powerful pumps.

more than slave labour, expected to work in extremely dangerous conditions and often treated appallingly. The OT even had its own armed security element in the form of various Schutzkommando, and even a Polizei Regiment Todt. After the fall of France and the Low Countries, a separate Todt element was set up to control construction in these occupied territories. The Organisation Todt-Einsatzgruppe West was based in Paris, under the command of Oberbaudirektor Karl Weis. The Einsatzgruppe was subdivided into a number of command areas (Oberbauleitung) many of which took direct responsibility for the construction of U-Boat bunkers in their areas. Following the death of Fritz Todt in 1942, control of the OT was handed to Albert Speer who severed the links with the DAF.

The Organisation Todt was closely linked with the DAF (Deutsche Arbeits Front), the official Nazi state trade union which had forcibly absorbed all independent trade unions and labour associations. Initially at least, relations between the German construction workers and local French labour hired to work on the projects were good. French workers and those brought in from other European countries were well fed, well paid and accommodated in a reasonable standard of comfort. There were even Spanish communists among them who had fled to France during the Spanish Civil War and had been interned. When the Germans invaded, these communists fell into their hands. Although they were, effectively, forced labour they were good workers and earned the respect of the Germans for their skills. This brought them relatively

One of the reasons the Germans were so successful in the construction of their U-Boat bunkers was the use of round-the-clock work. Here the site at Bordeaux is shown during night work. The site is illuminated by huge lights. In some cases searchlights were even used, bouncing the light off low cloud to reflect back on to the ground. Unfortunately this made the site an attractive target for enemy aircraft and following a warning that the enemy was approaching the lights would be switched off. Many workers, most of whom were there as forced labour, lost their lives in accidents when such sites were plunged into sudden darkness.

Pens at the massive Keroman complex at Lorient under construction, watched over by an armed sentry. This was the biggest and most successful of all U-Boat bunker sites, with much of it still being in use today.

good treatment from their captors. In Norway, however, Soviet prisoners of war were put to work and their treatment was far less satisfactory. Worst of all was the treatment of the concentration camp inmates put to work on projects such as the Valentin bunker near Bremen.

The German firms actually involved were many. Famous construction concerns such as Siemens-Bau-Union and Holzmann AG were responsible for the concrete work, whilst electrical installations were provided principally by Siemens-Schuckert. Machine manufacturing giants M.A.N. (Maschinenfabrik Augsburg-Nürnberg) provided the powerful pumping mechanisms required to fill and drain the concrete pens and dry docks. In addition, much work was subcontracted to local firms. In some cases over 15,000 workers might be employed at any one time on the construction of one of the major U-Boat bunkers.

Construction workers were employed in 12-hour shifts starting or ending at 7am or 7pm: work was thus kept going around the clock. Huge arc lights and even searchlights were used to illuminate the site at night and allow work to continue. Only when the air raid warnings sounded did work cease, albeit temporarily.

It is not entirely surprising that when selecting sites on which to erect the bunkers, existing French naval dockyards were often chosen (for example, Brest and Lorient): such locations were tidal and emerged into the open sea. Others were non-tidal (among them, St Nazaire, Bordeaux, and La Pallice) and built in existing civilian harbours. Access to the basins containing the bunkers was through lock gates.

RIGHT **Building the Valentin complex at Bremen**
This illustration shows the construction of the massive Valentin factory bunker near Bremen, near to the village of Farge. The second largest bunker to be built, it covered just over 49,000m$^2$ of ground on the northern bank of the River Weser. Almost a quarter of a million tons of concrete were used in its construction, as well as 27,000 tons of steel. The structure was erected at a total cost of 120,000,000 RM (Reichsmarks). Construction came under the control of the Marineoberbauleitung Weser, which authorised the creation of two construction co-operatives (Arbeitsgemeinschaften – abbreviated to ARGE). ARGE Nord consisted of the firms Lenzbau, Wayss & Freytag, Hochtief and Tesch, whilst ARGE Süd consisted of the firms Hermann Möller, Kögel and August Reiners. As the names imply, each of the co-operatives was responsible for construction work in either the northern or southern parts of the site. Consultant to the project was Professor Dr Arnold Agatz, one of the foremost experts on harbour construction and who also acted as a consultant to the bunker construction programme in France.

Completion was scheduled for the early part of 1945, though Hitler insisted that this should be brought forward to the second half of 1944. However, by the end of hostilities in May 1945, the complex was still not in service, despite being 90 per cent complete.

Railway lines were laid to the very centre of the complex, carrying materials straight through the bunker as it grew. A cement-mixing plant was also erected next to the bunker, to feed the project's insatiable appetite for concrete. The site resisted attempts by the Allies to destroy it with Tallboy and Grand-slam bombs: parts of it are still in use today.

One thing that marked the Valentin project out for special attention was the sheer volume of slave labour used during its construction. Over 10,000 forced labourers, prisoners of war and concentration camp inmates were used on the project. (As with the construction projects in France, there were some volunteers within the workforce.) A scale of charges was levied on the construction firms for the use of this manpower, running from 0.30 RM per day for a camp inmate, 0.40 RM per day for Soviet prisoners of war, up to 0.70 RM per day for West European workers. Over 4,000 members of the workforce lost their lives during the construction of the Valentin bunker.

Once the sites had been chosen, the preparatory work involved was enormous. The sites were cleared, and construction began by digging out the foundations and driving in the massive steel piles. Huge cofferdams were built to hold back the sea while the sites for the pens were excavated below water level. During the ongoing excavation work, the concrete floors would be laid on the site at the rear of the pens where the various workshop areas were to be positioned, and the steel reinforcements for the walls would be prepared, ready for the shuttering to be erected and the concrete for the walls to be poured in.

Enormous quantities of materials were needed for the construction of these bunkers, with thousands of square metres of concrete being poured every day once construction work was in full swing. The principal materials, steel and cement, were both (initially at least) transported all the way from Germany. The cement was packed in countless small 50kg paper sacks, and such vast quantities of paper were used for these that it was considered necessary to recycle the empty sacks. Later, loose cement was loaded into railway trucks and shipped by the wagonload. The cement was sprayed with water, dampening the top layer and thus forming a crust that would prevent the cement from being blown away. Still the quantities needed to feed the massive construction projects were so vast that materials began to be sourced locally, where suppliers could meet the German quality standards. Huge quantities of gravel and other ballast materials were also transported to the construction sites.

Railway tracks were laid to allow the hundreds of thousands of tons of steel, cement and, most importantly, sand to be carried right onto the site. The huge amounts of concrete required for one of these mammoth structures required equally huge quantities of sand, so much so that this in turn required even more miles of railway track to move the sand from the shore to the building site. Materials were also transported to the site by sea using barges and lighters, and by road in countless trucks.

## Bunker design

As well as providing shelter for the U-Boats themselves, the bunkers contained repair workshops, power generating plants (general power was drawn from the local electricity supply but diesel generator plants were provided to produce power in emergencies should the local supply be knocked out), pumping stations, storage facilities, offices, accommodation, ventilation units, heating units, telephone and communication rooms and first aid posts. Narrow-gauge rail tracks also ran into the bunkers themselves to allow heavy equipment to be

The Dora II site in Norway. Like many other sites of the second phase of bunker construction, this new complex competed for essential materials and manpower with other equally important construction projects. As a result, it was never fully completed, although work did reach a fairly advanced stage as can be seen here.

brought inside and to the U-Boats. For safety's sake, munitions such as torpedoes were generally stored away from the U-Boat pens in their own well-protected bunkers and brought into the complex when needed, by means of the narrow-gauge tracks.

The pens themselves were constructed in two styles, 'wet' and 'dry'. Dry pens were those capable of being pumped out and effectively used as dry-dock facilities for submarines requiring repair and maintenance. The actual dimensions of the pens varied, but as a general rule, the distance from the base of the pen to the level of the quay allowed for approximately 10m water depth, with a similar distance from quay level to ceiling. The height of the ceiling had to allow the overhead cranes to remove the periscopes fully from their housing for repair or replacement. The quayside was normally around 1.5m wide.

Each pen had at least one overhead crane running down its length. These had capacities ranging from one ton up to thirty tons, the U-Boat being directed into whichever pen had a crane or cranes of the requisite capacity for the work required. Each pen was served by main pumps with a 3,000m³ capacity and smaller auxiliary drainage pumps with a 380m³ capacity. These pumps were located at pumping stations between each pen, usually with two of each of these pumps per station. This was by no means a universal arrangement, but it was by far the most typical set-up: some bases had all the pumping equipment located in the service areas in the main block behind the pens themselves. These powerful pumps took anything from three hours upwards to empty a pen completely and create a dry-dock facility.

Protection for the pen interiors was provided by massive armoured steel plates, some up to a metre thick. These could be in the form of steel shutters, which were lowered vertically from above the entrance to the pen, or conventional hinged doors. These armoured plates would in some cases extend down to the level of the quay (for dry pens) whilst others only provided cover for some two-thirds of the opening, leaving just under two metres of the entrance open. Some of the protective doors to the bunker complexes were hollow boxes made from thick plate, which were then filled with concrete.

Given the Kriegsmarine's urgent need for protected repair facilities for their U-Boats, the dry-dock capable pens were generally the first to be constructed. It was common for the first pens to be put into use as soon as they were ready, whilst the remaining pens were still under construction.

With the greatest threat to these bunkers coming from enemy aircraft, it is no surprise that the most innovative development work was carried out on the design of the bunker roof. The result of this was the creation of roofs that were virtually impregnable.

Here we see the huge steel arches that supported the roof being manoeuvred into place at the Valentin bunker at Bremen-Farge. Concrete was then poured over this framework to provide immense structural strength.

The rear end of the Valentin bunker, containing the various workshop areas, under construction. One of the roof-supporting arches (top left) has been partially encased in its concrete shell. Just below this can be seen the floor of the topmost workshop level.

## Protected locks

As several of the U-Boat bunkers were located in basins in the inner harbour of their port, access would normally be via a set of lock gates. Though the bunker complexes themselves were immensely strong, the unprotected locks were definite weak spots. If these were put out of action, boats would be unable to enter or leave their pens. In order to protect this Achilles heel, especially after the British attack on the lock at St Nazaire, it was decided to enclose these locks in their own protective bunkers: St Nazaire, La Pallice and Bordeaux were all to have these. Effectively, these looked like miniature U-Boat bunkers. Though never completed at Bordeaux, the locks at St Nazaire and La Pallice still stand to this day. The partially completed lock at Bordeaux was demolished after the war.

At St Nazaire the lock was built a few yards along from the lock which gave access to the inner harbour via the Normandie dry dock, which was damaged when it was rammed during a commando raid by HMS *Campbeltown*. She was one of the old 'four-stacker' destroyers supplied by the USA under the lend-lease programme. After the destroyer was rammed into the lock gates, a huge cargo of explosives carried on board was detonated, destroying the gates.

The new protected lock was almost directly in front of pens 8 and 9 of the bunker complex. This lock, begun in August 1942, was some 155m long, 25m wide and 14m high. A roadway ran through the lock, entering via doors

The lock gate giving access to the inner port basin was also a weak spot, and any damage to this could cause serious disruption. After the attack on the lock gates at St Nazaire, which were rammed and destroyed by HMS *Campbeltown*, the Germans began a programme of erecting reinforced-concrete bunkers over the locks. Here we see the construction of the bunker over the lock at Lorient.

in its side, and crossed the lock waters by means of a bridge, which could be raised when a vessel passed through. The lock was capable of being pumped dry, and in addition to the intrinsic protection offered by the reinforced concrete roof and walls, had its own flak defences on the roof, with four emplacements for 2cm flak guns on a special platform on the western side. At La Pallice, the massive sheltered lock was 167m long, 26m wide and 14m high. It was not used until August 1944.

A number of fascinating new projects were planned, the most interesting of which was the proposal to turn the eastern portion of the Rove Tunnel at Marseilles (which opened out in the north-west part of the harbour at Port de la Lave) into a U-Boat bunker, suitable for handling the smaller Type XXIII coastal boats. It was also planned to build bunkers at Rügen, Gotenhafen and at Nikolajew in the Crimea, and to create additional bunker facilities at Kiel, Bremen and Hamburg.

The optical repair workshop inside the U-Boat pen at St Nazaire. Here repair and maintenance work was carried out primarily on U-Boat periscopes. Note the spare periscopes on the wall racks.

# Tour of a U-Boat base

Each bunker complex was subtly different to its counterparts in its layout: however, there were a number of standard features. The example we will use here to tour the layout of a bunker site, namely the complex at Brest, will illustrate most of the common features found in all the operational sites.

When the Germany Army, in the form of 5 Panzer Division, occupied the port of Brest in June 1940, it was only to discover that the withdrawing British troops had destroyed most of the port facilities. The Germans began urgent repair works immediately and within two months the first of Dönitz's U-Boats, *U-65* under the command of Kapitänleutnant von Stockhausen, entered Brest for repairs. By the middle of the following month, the port of Brest was fully functional once more.

Almost immediately, preparations began for the establishment of an operational U-Boat base. Construction of protective concrete pens began in January 1941 and lasted for approximately nine months. The layout actually consisted of two bunkers in one. The first contained five wet pens, 115m long and 17m wide, each capable of accommodating up to three boats: the second contained eight dry repair pens 99m long and 11m wide, and a further two 114m long and 13m wide, each capable of accommodating just one boat. Overall, the bunker measured 333m in length and 192m in width, and its height was 17m.

The first U-Boats to arrive at Brest were from Unterseebootsflotille 1 Weddigen, transferring from Kiel in June 1941, followed four months later by Unterseebootsflotille 9. The first recorded use of the U-Boat pens was in September 1941, though the complex was not fully completed until the summer of 1942.

The harbour at Brest was bounded by a protective mole (a harbour wall), the bunker being tucked in the eastern corner of the harbour, with the mole emerging from the eastern side of the bunker. The forward part of the bunker,

An aerial view of the Brest complex taken in the mid-1970s. This gives an excellent view of the bunker roof with its partially installed *Fangrost* support beams.

A flak gun emplacement on the roof of the Scorff bunker at Lorient.

Bombers however, having survived enemy fighter attacks, and the heavy anti-aircraft fire around the port areas, would in almost every case find that the bombs they dropped had a negligible effect on the bunkers themselves, though collateral damage to the harbour areas and even the towns themselves was often severe. The bombers would then have to run the gauntlet of further fighter attacks as they made for home. In most cases, expending huge resources in terms of fuel and munitions and losing both aircraft and aircrew would have resulted in little or no damage to the U-Boat bunker. Low-flying aircraft would have a better chance of evading enemy fighters and avoiding anti-aircraft fire, but would be lucky to inflict any major damage unless they intercepted a U-Boat on the surface either leaving or returning to the bunker.

In essence therefore, the U-Boat bunker can be considered a defensive triumph, with most of them surviving the war virtually intact despite numerous enemy attacks. A few boats received damage from falling masonry inside the bunkers but this was nothing compared to the potential damage which might have been caused to boats moored in open, unprotected basins. The U-Boat war was lost at sea, as Allied anti-submarine measures took an ever-increasing toll on German submarines and trained crews. The bunkers themselves, however, provided a safe haven for exhausted boats and their crews to the bitter end.

**Defending the base from low-flying aircraft**

This illustration shows a typical low-level attack by enemy aircraft on a bunker complex. Smaller single- or twin-engined aircraft, travelling at low altitude and at much greater speed than their heavier four-engined counterparts, had a much better chance of avoiding detection by enemy radar and aircraft spotters. The downside was that their payload was much smaller, though torpedo-carrying aircraft could inflict considerable damage if their payload entered one of the pen openings. Although the massive pen itself would suffer little damage, any U-Boat inside would probably be destroyed.

A number of defensive measures were taken against such low-flying aircraft, several of which can be seen here. On the roof of the bunker are a number of concrete emplacements equipped with the four-barrel 2cm Flakvierling (**1**). With each barrel capable of firing up to 450 rounds per minute, each mount had a combined rate of fire of 1,800 rounds per minute. Multiply this by the number of mounts on the bunker roof, all firing at once, and it can be seen that if all three concentrated their fire on a single attacker, the pilot would face a daunting barrage. He would certainly have to manoeuvre

sharply to avoid being hit, and would therefore reduce his chances of maintaining a course long enough to launch his weapon accurately.

In addition to the anti-aircraft weapons on the bunker itself, any important military base such as a harbour complex would be bristling with other anti-aircraft weapons of varying calibre, adding to the weight of fire being thrown against enemy aircraft. It is estimated, for example, that when the port at Lorient finally surrendered a total of 287 flak guns were seized. These ranged from light 2cm flak for use against low-flying aircraft, to massive twin 10.5cm and 12.8cm guns for use against high-altitude bombers.

In addition, the pilot would have to avoid the cables of barrage balloons anchored to vessels in the harbour near to the bunker (**2**), as well as extended masts fitted to such ships to provide further hazards for low-flying aircraft (**3**).

An anti-torpedo net drawn across the harbour in front of the pens (**4**) would provide yet another obstacle to a successful strike. Taking all these factors into account, it is understandable that light attack aircraft scored even fewer successes against the U-Boat bunkers than the heavy bombers did.

The side wall of the St Nazaire bunker. The figure to the bottom right gives some idea of the sheer size of this amazing structure. Like most of the French bunkers, it is in surprisingly good condition. (Chris Boonzaier)

# Life in a U-Boat base

Each of the French and Norwegian U-Boat bunker complexes hosted at least one and in some cases two U-Boat flotillas. These flotillas were basically fixed command structures to which individual boats were allocated. Boats could be, and indeed often were, re-allocated to other flotillas over a period of time. Each flotilla commander was himself an experienced U-Boat commander, and indeed many of them were top aces who, having served their time in combat, were promoted and re-assigned to a shore posting, ensuring that their vast experience would survive to be handed on to those who followed.

The U-Boat arm was initially commanded by Konteradmiral Karl Dönitz. On the fall of France, Dönitz made his headquarters in Paris, but in September 1940 transferred to a luxurious mansion at Kerneval. The growing threat of enemy attack, not only from the air but also in the form of commando raids (especially after the events at St Nazaire) saw Hitler insist in March 1942 that he relocate back to Paris. On being promoted to Grossadmiral and Commander-in-Chief Navy, Dönitz retained his passionate interest in the welfare and performance of his U-Boats and was often on hand at the U-Boat bases in France to welcome home his Grey Wolves after a successful war cruise.

Head of Operations under Dönitz was Kapitän zur See Eberhardt Godt, while the post of Head of Organisation was held by Kapitän zur See Hans-Georg von Friedeburg. The individual operational areas into which the U-Boat force was divided were each commanded by a Flag Officer. The post of Führer der U-Boote West, based in Paris and covering the areas of operation in which most of the boats from the French U-Boat bunker complexes operated, was held by Kapitän zur See Hans-Rudolf Rösing from its inception in July 1942 through to May 1945.

In general, U-Boats operating from the Norwegian bunkers came under the control of the Führer der U-Boote Norwegen, based in Narvik. This post was held by Kapitän zur See Rudolf Peters from January 1943 to May 1944 and then by Fregattenkapitän Reinhard Sühren from May 1944 until May 1945. It should be stressed that it was the area in which the boats were to operate that determined which Flag Officer would be responsible, rather than the area in which their home port lay.

Efforts were made to rotate U-Boat crews. On return from a gruelling war patrol, the boat would tie up in the bunker and the majority of the crew would be granted home leave. A train was often laid on by order of Dönitz as B.d.U. (Befehlshaber der U-Boote) or C-in-C U-Boats to ensure that the crews were transported home to Germany as quickly as possible and that as little of their precious leave as possible was lost in travelling. This train was known as the B.d.U.-Zug or C-in-C's train.

Meanwhile a skeleton crew would stay with their boat, carrying out routine maintenance work. The crews were normally accommodated in barracks some way away from the bunker complex for safety's sake given the risk of (albeit ineffectual) Allied air raids. There was, however, a substantial amount of accommodation space within the bunker complex in which personnel could be housed if necessary. Very occasionally, crewmen engaged in maintenance work might actually sleep onboard their boat in the bunker. In some cases, training facilities were even added to the bunker complex, an example of this being the 7m tank built onto the side of the Keroman I bunker and used for training U-Boat crews in underwater escape drill (see Warrior 36 *Grey Wolf: U-Boat Crewman of World War II*).

During wartime, the U-Boat bunker was a busy site. With one third of the fleet on operational duty, another third in transit to and from operational areas, and the remaining third in port, it would be a rare occasion when the bunker was found to be totally empty. Boats in port would be undergoing repair and maintenance, refuelling, re-arming, restocking food and other supplies, and generally airing the boat to remove the inevitable smell of several weeks at sea with 50 unwashed sailors. Water was far too precious a commodity to use for washing.

During the so-called 'Happy Times', the period of U-Boat dominance early in the Battle of the Atlantic, bunkers would regularly witness the arrival of their resident U-Boats after successful missions, bedecked with victory pennants representing numerous ships sunk as the U-Boats ran amok amongst the poorly protected merchant ships. Bands would play on the dockside and female auxiliaries would wait with garlands of flowers ready to hang around the neck of the returning ace.

As the French ports that housed the U-Boat bunkers were to find out, U-Boat men lived hard, and played hard. Those crew members who had to remain with their boat made the most of their off-duty time and lost no opportunity to paint the town red. The Military Police (Feldgendarmerie) had to work hard to keep them in check. Some very fine hotels, even small *chateaux*, were taken over as accommodation for U-Boat crews in these French bases. Local cinemas showed German films and theatres put on German plays. U-Boat crewmen were also provided with superior rations – small recompense for the dangers they faced. In general, the local French population was polite in its relations with the Germans though this deteriorated as the fortunes of war turned against Germany, especially after the Allied landings in Normandy.

U-Boat bases were also home to a large number of administrative personnel, or *Marine Beamten*. These men, mostly officers but with a small number of senior NCOs, wore naval uniform but with silver rather than the traditional gold insignia, and were generally reviled by the sailors who referred to them contemptuously as *Silberlings*. These administrative personnel were directly attached to the U-Boat flotillas, but generally had little or no sea-going experience (though photographic evidence shows a few individuals wearing the U-Boat War Badge, indicating that they at least had served at the front).

This shot shows a Type IX which, having been lined up with the receiving pen, is about to be winched backwards into the protective enclosure.

Many of them took a dim view of what they saw as a lack of discipline on the part of the U-Boat crews once they returned to port, and they were not beyond trying to throw their weight around, which of course did not go down well with the crews. These officials were responsible for handling pay, procuring supplies, and other such matters.

As the fortunes of war turned against the U-Boats, successes became more rare, and mere survival became a considerable achievement – and the U-Boat bunkers saw fewer and fewer celebrations. No longer were the quays packed with well-wishers: however the sight of these great concrete behemoths remained a welcome sight for the decreasing number of unscathed U-Boats returning from ever more dangerous war cruises.

# Resident flotillas and commanders in Europe

### Brest

Brest was home to 1 Unterseebootsflotille commanded variously by Korvettenkapitän Hans Eckermann (January–October 1940), Korvettenkapitän Hans Cohausz (November 1940–February 1942), Kapitänleutnant Heinz Buchholz (February 1942–July 1942) and Korvettenkapitän Werner Winter (July 1942–May 1945).

By the time the flotilla moved from its home port of Kiel to France, it had already replaced its small Type II boats with the Type VII and also operated a number of Type IX boats from the bunker complex in Brest. The port also hosted 9 Unterseebootsflotille, a wartime-raised unit equipped with the ubiquitous Type VII. This flotilla was commanded by Kapitänleutnant Jurgen Oesten (November 1941–March 1942) and Korvettenkapitän Heinrich Lehmann-Willenbrock (March 1942–August 1944).

Brest was home to, amongst others, great aces like Kapitänleutnant Reinhard Sühren and Kapitänleutnant Adalbert Schnee. Sühren, who served his 'apprenticeship' as a Watch Officer under Herbert Schultze in *U-48*, went on to command *U-564* and sank 18 ships totalling 95,000 tons, whilst Schnee, in *U-201*, accounted for 24 ships totalling some 89,000 tons.

### Lorient

2 Unterseebootsflotille moved from its home port of Wilhelmshaven to the Lorient base in France in the summer of 1940. The two operational examples of the large Type IA U-Boats served with this flotilla, though the bulk of its boats were Type VII and Type IX. Its commanders were Korvettenkapitän Werner Hartmann (January 1940–May 1940), Korvettenkapitän Heinz Fischer (June 1940–October 1940), Korvettenkapitän Viktor Schütze (October 1940–January 1943) and Fregattenkapitän Ernst Kals (January 1943–May 1945).

The U-Boat bunkers at Lorient also housed 10 Unterseebootsflotille, operating a mixture of Type IX, XB and XIV boats. It was commanded by Korvettenkapitän Günter Kuhnke (January 1942–October 1944).

LEFT **Inside a U-Boat bunker**
This ilustration shows the interior of a U-Boat bunker. An operational boat is undergoing repair and maintenance in one of the dry-dock-capable pens. These were generally intended to only accommodate one boat at a time, unlike the wet pens that could normally take at least two boats. The pen has been fully drained, but water would continue to leak in and so pumps were used to keep the pen as dry as possible. The U-Boat has been lowered onto the stocks, and engineers are examining a damaged propeller. This view gives a good impression of the depth of a typical pen. Note also the corrugated steel shuttering on the ceiling, the purpose of which was to prevent any masonry dislodged by a heavy-bomb direct hit from becoming dislodged and crashing down onto any boat within the pen. In most cases the quays between the pens would be around 6.3m wide, with a dividing wall running down the centre, thus allowing only a fairly narrow walkway around 2.5m wide each side. Looking up towards the ceiling, we can see the mobile gantry crane. The crane was used for tasks such as removing a damaged periscope from a U-Boat. Such operations explain why the pens had what might otherwise be seen as unnecessarily high ceilings.

The western side entrance to the U-Boat pens at Brest. The slogan reads 'Through struggle to victory'. The immense thickness of the steel door can clearly be seen: any attempt at forced entry would be a daunting prospect.

Aces such as Kapitänleutnant Fritz Julius Lemp in *U-30*, Kapitänleutnant Günther Prien in *U-47*, Kapitänleutnant Otto Kretschmer in *U-99* and Kapitänleutnant Joachim Schepke in *U-100* all sailed from Lorient, between them racking up a total of over 720,000 tons of enemy shipping sunk. Lorient was also home base for Kapitänleutnant Reinhard Hardegen, commander of *U-123*, who sank 24 enemy ships totalling 138,000 tons. Of course, U-Boats from time to time changed their commanders. Lorient, as well as playing host to some of the highest ranking aces, was also the home base to some of the most successful boats, *U-48*, *U-99*, *U-103*, *U-124* and *U-107*, the five highest scoring boats of the war.

### La Pallice

This French base was home to 3 Unterseebootsflotille which moved from its original home in Kiel after the fall of France. Once its elderly Type II boats had been phased out, it operated exclusively with Type VIIs. The flotilla was commanded by Korvettenkapitän Hans-Rudolf Rösing (March 1941–July 1941), Korvettenkapitän Herbert Schultze (July 1941–March 1942), Korvettenkapitän

Heinz von Reiche (March 1942–June 1942) and Korvettenkapitän Richard Zapp (June 1942–October 1944).

La Pallice was also home to many spectacularly successful aces, amongst them Kapitänleutnant 'Ali' Cremer of *U-333*, Kapitänleutnant Heinz Otto Schultze of *U-432* and Kapitänleutnant Siegfried von Forstner of *U-402* to name but three. These experts between them sank over 174,000 tons of enemy shipping.

## St Nazaire

This was the home of 6 Unterseebootsflotille, another flotilla which operated exclusively with the Type VII. Its original home had been the Baltic port of Danzig. The commanders of this flotilla were Korvettenkapitän Wilhelm Schulz (September 1941–October 1943) and Korvettenkapitän Carl Emmermann (October 1943–August 1944).

St Nazaire hosted two of the war's most famous boats; *U-96* with its distinctive 'laughing swordfish' emblem, under Kapitänleutnant Heinrich Lehmann-Willenbrock, with 25 ships totalling 183,250 tons to his credit; and the 'Red Devil Boat', *U-552* under the command of Kapitänleutnant Erich Topp, destroyer of 35 ships totalling some 192,600 tons.

## Bordeaux

Bordeaux was home to 12 Unterseebootsflotille as well as a number of Italian U-Boats. The German boats operating from this port were a mixture of Type IX and Type XIVs under the command of Korvettenkapitän Klaus Scholz (October 1942–August 1944).

Although Bordeaux was better known initially as a base for Italian submarines and the so-called *Milch Kuh* supply submarines, it also boasted its own ace, the phenomenally successful Korvettenkapitän Wolfgang Lüth. Lüth, in command of *U-181*, sank a grand total of 47 ships totalling over 221,000 tons, making him the most successful U-Boat commander of World War II and earning him the Knight's Cross with Oakleaves, Swords and Diamonds.

## Trondheim

The bunkers at this Norwegian port were home to 13 Unterseebootsflotille under the command of Fregattenkapitän Rolf Rüggenberg (June 1943–May 1945). It was equipped with Type VIIC boats. Amongst the aces who operated from Trondheim were Kapitänleutnant Max-Martin Teichert, commander of *U-456*, who sank the cruiser HMS *Edinburgh*; Kapitänleutnant Hans-Günther Lange of *U-711*, an Oakleaves winner who sank the British destroyer HMS *Ashanti*; Oberleutnant Otto Westphalen, commander of *U-968*, who included three enemy warships in his total score; and Kapitänleutnant Paul Brasak, commander of *U-737*.

## Bergen

The U-Boat bunkers at Bergen housed the boats of 11 Unterseebootsflotille, equipped with the Type VIIC. This flotilla was commanded by Fregattenkapitän Hans Cohausz (May 1942–January 1945) and Fregattenkapitän Heinrich Lehmann-Willenbrock (January 1945–May 1945).

Aces sailing from Bergen included Kapitänleutnant Heinrich Schroeteler, Kapitänleutnant Rolf Thomsen, commander of *U-1202*, and also highly experienced ace commanders such as Kapitänleutnant Karl-Heinz Franke, Kapitänleutnant Horst von Schroeter, Korvettenkapitän Adalbert Schnee and Korvettenkapitän Peter 'Ali' Cremer, who had all been given commands with the new Type XXI U-Boat.

## Kiel

Home of 1, 3, 5 and 7 U-Boat flotillas. All of these moved into bases in occupied Europe after the outbreak of war. No bunkers were erected for these flotillas.

The interior of the Bruno bunker in Bergen. The U-Boats of the Kriegsmarine have been replaced by the submarines of the Royal Norwegian Navy. (Photo courtesy Hans Lauritzen)

Pre-war photos tend to show the U-Boats simply tied up alongside their depot ship. 1, 3 and 7 flotillas came under the command of Führer der U-Boote West whilst 5 U-Boat Flotilla came under command of Führer der U-Boote Ost.

### Wilhelmshaven
This port was home to 2, 6, 22 and 31 U-Boat flotillas, though 22 and 31 used Wilhelmshaven only in the latter part of the war. 2, 6 and 31 U-Boat flotillas came under the command of Führer der U-boote Ost. 22 U-Boat Flotilla came under the command of 2 Unterseebootslehrdivision.

### Pillau
This port, on the Bay of Danzig, was one of the bases from which several of the U-Boat training flotillas operated. For most of the war, the Baltic was firmly under German control and its waters were relatively safe for inexperienced crews undergoing training. At various times, Pillau was home to 19, 20, 21 and 26 U-Boat flotillas.

### Gotenhafen
On the western side of the Bay of Danzig, Gotenhafen was variously home to 22, 24, 25 and 27 U-Boat flotillas: all were training flotillas. It was also the base port of 2 U-Bootlehrdivision.

### Hela
On the Baltic, near Gotenhafen, Hela was a training base for U-Boats but had no permanently assigned flotillas.

### Danzig
23, 24 and 25 U-Boat flotillas operated from this port. It was the final home of 23 U-Boat Flotilla, from August 1943 until the end of the war, specialising in

training crews in underwater torpedo firing. All three flotillas were training units. Danzig was also the base of the Führer der Unterseeboote Ost.

In addition to the bases already listed, U-Boat bases were established at the following locations.

| Memel | In the eastern Baltic, Memel was but one of the temporary homes of 25 U-Boat Flotilla, and was also home base for 4 U-Bootlehrdivision. |
| --- | --- |
| Libau | To the north of Memel, Libau was another of the temporary homes for 25 U-Boat Flotilla. |
| Neustadt | This port, in Schleswig-Holstein, was not an operational base, but was home to 1 and 3 U-Bootlehrdivision. |
| Travemünde | To the north-east of Hamburg, this Baltic port was also at one point home to 25 U-Boat Flotilla. |
| Eckernförde | Just north of the eastern end of the Kiel Canal, Eckernförde was an important naval base, the waters off this port being used for ship speed trials. It was also the final home of 24 U-Boat Flotilla. |
| Warnemünde | Just north of the major port of Rostock, this base was the final home of 26 U-Boat Flotilla. |
| Königsberg | The East Prussian city was briefly home to 32 U-Boat Flotilla before it moved to Hamburg when the city was threatened by the Soviet advance. The flotilla came under the command of Führer der U-Boote Ost. |
| Flensburg | Flensburg, adjacent to the Naval Academy at Mürwik, and opening onto the Geltinger Bay, was home to 33 U-Boat Flotilla, though boats from this flotilla spent much of their time in the Far East. This flotilla came under the command of Führer der U-Boote West. |
| Horten | On the southern coast of Norway, Horten was a base dedicated to training and repair facilities. It was not home to any specific flotilla. |
| Narvik | Though not a U-Boat base as such, this sea port in the far north of Norway was the command base of the Führer der Unterseeboote Norwegen. |
| La Spezia, Pola, and Salamis | La Spezia in north-west Italy, Pola, on the Adriatic near Italy's border with Yugoslavia, and the Greek port of Salamis all played host to 29 U-Boat Flotilla, a large operational unit with up to 54 boats under its control. This flotilla also used the French ports of Toulon and Marseilles. Boats operating from these bases came under the command of Führer der Unterseeboote Mittelmeer. |
| Constanza and Feodosia | Constanza on the Black Sea and the Crimean port of Feodosia were the main operational bases of 30 U-Boat Flotilla. |

# Bases in the Pacific and the Far East

Once Japan entered the war, the Germans received several requests to send boats into the Indian Ocean, but these requests were politely ignored, the Kriegsmarine's U-Boats being fully occupied in the Atlantic. However, as the tide of war began to turn against the U-Boats, and pickings in the Atlantic became harder to find, the possibilities of success in the Far East became more attractive. With Allied countermeasures believed to be weak in these waters, Dönitz despatched a group of Type IX boats, known as the 'Monsun' boats, to seek fresh success in these far-off waters. U-Boats operating in the Far East came under the command of Fregattenkapitän Wilhelm Dommes as Chef der U-Boote im Südraum. Dommes was based in Penang.

| Penang | A small number of bases were provided by the Imperial Japanese Navy, the most important of these being at Penang on the western side of the Malay Peninsula. German boats began to operate from this port in July 1943. |
| --- | --- |
| Singapore | Additional facilities, specifically for repair and maintenance work, were established at Singapore in the summer of 1944. These remained in use until Germany's surrender in May 1945. |
| Batavia | This Indonesian port was the site of a further small repair and maintenance base for U-Boats operating in the Far East. |
| Kobe | This Japanese port was host to a small U-Boat facility that was established specifically for repairing U-Boat batteries plus general repair work. |

# Bunkers, bombs and raids – the bases at war

## Hamburg

### Elbe II

Plans for a new U-Boat bunker at the Howaldtswerke yards on the River Elbe at Hamburg were approved in 1940, with construction commencing at the end of that year. Erected by the firm of Dyckerhoff & Widmann AG at the east end of the Vulkan basin, the bunker was completed in March 1941 and consisted of two pens. Each pen was 112m in length and 22.5m in width and could accommodate three boats moored side by side.

To the rear of the bunker at ground level were a storage area on the west side, and offices and electrical switch-gear on the eastern side. The entire upper floor of this rear area was fitted out with workbenches and various equipment such as drills, vertical and horizontal boring machines, and lathes. Landward access was via small, well-protected steel doors on each side of the bunker.

The Elbe II bunker was used primarily to provide cover for new Type XXI U-Boats being fitted out, and for existing boats returning to the yard for refit or repair. Despite numerous Allied bombing raids, the boats in the interior of the bunker remained safe, though some damage to the roof of the structure was achieved. On the night of 8 March 1945 a force of over 300 RAF bombers attacked the Hamburg dock area, dropping almost 1,000 tons of bombs. This was only the start of a concentrated bombing campaign against the dock installations in Hamburg. At the end of March, the RAF returned with a force of over 450 bombers and dropped over 2,200 tons of bombs on the area, laying waste to the Howaldtswerke yards but doing little or no damage to the bunker. The massive hanging steel doors covering the entrance were blown off during an air raid on 8 April 1945, when once again over 400 bombers attacked the area.

Six submarines, *U-2505*, *U-3004*, *U-2501* and *U-3506* (all Type XXIs) plus *U-684* and *U-685* (Type VIICs), were sheltering in the Elbe II bunker when the war ended. The Type XXIs were all awaiting repair and the Type VIICs were not fully completed. All six boats were crammed into the westernmost pen.

The Elbe II bunker at Hamburg. Although consisting of only two pens, it was still a sizeable structure. On the roof of the bunker various office and workshop facilities were built. A Type VII U-Boat is moored beside the bunker.

Following the German agreement to surrender the city of Hamburg to British forces on 3 May, the crews of the Type XXIs made immediate preparations to scuttle their boats using explosive charges. *U-3506*, *U-3004* and *U-2505* were scuttled inside the pen, the others were moved out into the harbour waters before being sunk.

## Fink II

The Fink II bunker, the largest to be built on German soil, was also constructed at Hamburg. Erected at the Deutsche Werft yards at Hamburg Finkenwerder, the main contractors involved were Wayss & Freytag and Beton & Monierbau AG. Although plans were approved in 1940, work did not commence until March 1941.

The bunker was actually built on dry land at the Deutsche Werfte yards, then a large triangular area of ground between it and the inlet from the River Elbe was excavated and the resulting area flooded. The structure consisted initially of four pens, all at just over 111m in length. The first was 27.5m in width, and the three remaining pens each 22.5m in width. A fifth pen was approved in September 1942 with construction beginning in May 1943 and completion in April 1944. This fifth pen, like the first, was 27.5m in width. Overall dimensions of the bunker were 153m in width and 139m in length.

The fifth pen was built slightly higher than the original pens, so that its roof could be supported by the edge of the original fourth pen. To the rear of the first four pens was a work area stretching back a further 20m: this same area behind the final, fifth pen stretched back for 39.5m.

The bunker could accommodate up to 15 boats, with three side by side in each pen. Landward access was by a single door on the west side of the bunker and a double door on the east. To the rear, on the east side of the projecting fifth pen was a further single entrance door.

As with Elbe II, the Fink II bunker was intended primarily to give shelter to U-Boats constructed at the adjacent yards whilst fitting out or being repaired or refitted. Protection against low-level bombing was provided by three 3.7cm flak positions on the bunker roof.

The bunker did not suffer any particularly serious bombing raids until April 1945 when it suffered two separate attacks. The first, on 4 April, was a daylight raid carried out by US bombers with special armour-piercing bombs, and caused little or no damage. The second, on 9 April, was carried out by 17 Lancaster bombers carrying the massive five-ton Tallboy bombs, as well as two of the

An aerial view of the Fink II bunker complex (arrowed). The area surrounding the bunker is heavily cratered, but the bunker itself remains virtually intact despite direct hits.

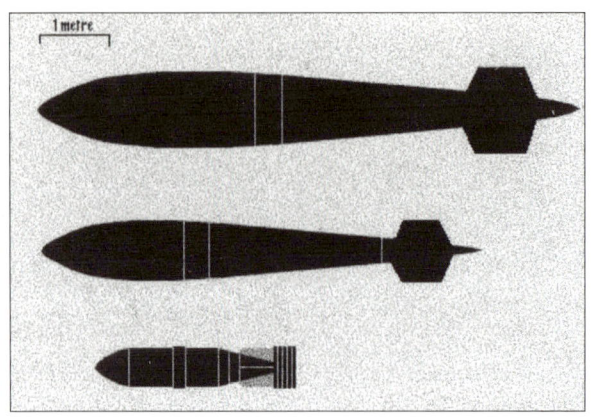

ABOVE LEFT
Top: a Grand-slam bomb. Middle: a Tallboy bomb.
Bottom: the standard German 1,000kg bomb.

ABOVE RIGHT Bunker-busting bombs: the Tallboy is to the left and the Grand-slam bomb is to the right in this picture taken at RAF Lossiemouth, UK.

Grand-slam 10-ton bombs. Of the 17 bombs dropped, six hit the bunker. The roof of the bunker was actually penetrated, but it was the pressure wave from the explosion that caused the greatest damage. A number of Type XXIII boats inside received minor damage, whilst the floating dry dock containing two boats in the new fifth pen sank: the boats inside, *U-677* and *U-982*, although submerged, remained relatively undamaged. The massive structure survived though and ended the war virtually intact.

# Helgoland

### Nordsee III

Helgoland was a long-established German naval base and a logical spot for the construction of a U-Boat bunker. Plans were drawn up as early as 1939 and by 1940 work was well under way: construction was completed in June 1941. The principal contractor for excavation work was Grün & Bilfinger and for actual construction the Hamburg firm of Dyckerhoff & Widmann AG was selected.

The bunker was a fairly modest one, lying in the east basin of the harbour on Helgoland. It comprised only three pens, all of which were wet pens: each could accommodate three submarines. A floating dry dock was also provided which could be towed into one of the pens should dry repair facilities be required. The dry dock could accommodate only a single submarine.

The bunker was 156m in length and 94m in width, each pen being approximately 108m long and 22m wide, with a 6m-wide quay separating each pen. The roof was some 3m thick and the walls 2m thick. To the rear of the easternmost pen lay a workshop for periscopes and optical equipment as

The Fink II bunker at the end of hostilities, the waters surrounding it filled with the detritus of war including a number of wrecked U-Boats.

The island of Helgoland, site of numerous defensive structures, including a modestly sized U-Boat bunker.

*U-134* about to enter the bunker at Helgoland.

well as torpedo storage, whilst to the rear of the westernmost pen was a workshop area with welding facilities and also an oxygen tank storage area and a carpenters' workshop.

Of less importance to the U-Boat war than many other bunker complexes, Nordsee III did not come in for much attention from Allied bombers until late in the war. There were no resident flotillas, and once the French and Norwegian bases fell into German hands, Nordsee III saw only 'passing trade' with boats calling in for repair or resupply. In fact, the U-Boat bunkers were used just as often, if not more often, to shelter small surface craft such as E-Boats.

After the Allied landings in Normandy in June 1944, the Nordsee III bunker became a staging point for the *Seehund*-type midget submarines under Vizeadmiral Heye, on their way from Wilhelmshaven to the invasion front, and at one point even housed a number of so-called *Sprengboote*. These were small motor boats packet with explosives which were driven directly at their targets, the operator leaping overboard at the last possible moment and being picked up by a control boat.

Defences on the bunker itself were fairly light, comprising just two 3.7cm flak guns and one 2cm flak gun together with a 2m searchlight. From late-1944, however, both the USAAF and RAF began to mount raids against the Helgoland base. A total of six major raids were launched against the complex between 1941 and 1945, the RAF raid on 18 April 1945 involving over 960 bombers. A final raid on the following day saw just 36 bombers drop 22 Tallboy bombs. The U-Boat bunker suffered no significant damage in any of these attacks and was still completely intact at the end of the war.

# Kiel

### Kilian

Sited on the east bank of Kiel harbour, the relatively small Kilian bunker was built during the winter of 1941/42 to provide protection for newly built U-Boats before they were allocated to their operational flotillas, as well as for the repair of operational and training boats.

Two pens were provided, separated by an internal dividing wall, each 138m long and 23m wide, allowing two boats to be accommodated one behind the other with three side by side. The bunker could therefore accommodate a total of 12 boats at full capacity. On the north-west (front) corner of the bunker was a small concrete tower to accommodate a flak gun position. Only a relatively small area of the bunker was allocated to workshop space, though this was spread over three floors (ground and two upper floors).

The overall length of the bunker was 176m, with walls just over 3m thick and a 4.8m-thick roof. Protection for the interior was provided by seven thick, hanging, overlapping steel plates forming a door, which reached down to water level. There was no special protection below water level.

The bunker was finally completed on 13 November 1943, having taken around one year to construct. *U-1101*, a Type VIIc became the first U-Boat to enter the bunker. The labour force consisted of well over a thousand men, working around the clock in two shifts, and comprising to a large degree forced labourers, camp inmates and prisoners of war. The death rate amongst the workers for whom no provision for shelter was made during bombing raids was extremely high.

The principal contractor for the construction of Kilian was the firm of Dyckerhoff & Widmann AG. Initially, the bunker escaped the attentions of the Allies, and general raids on Kiel harbour facilities saw Kilian remain unscathed. On 9 April 1945 however, a massive bombing raid, which sank the pocket battleship *Admiral Scheer*, saw the protective doors of the bunker blown off by a near miss. Inside the bunker at this time were two U-Boats, *U-170* (not a new boat, but being used as a test-bed) and *U-4708*. So great was the pressure wave from the bomb blast that the small Type XXIII *U-4708* was lifted into the air and smashed against the side of the pen causing such damage that she sank almost immediately. The larger and more robust *U-170* escaped destruction. The concrete structure of the bunker remained intact and survived the war. The last few U-Boats resident within were scuttled or blown up at the end of the war.

### Konrad

This bunker was in fact a conversion of an existing facility, namely the Dry Dock III of the Deutsche-Werke construction yard. Work commenced in April

The Kilian bunker at the end of the war, just before its demolition by troops from the Royal Engineers.

1943, the intention being to provide shelter for boats undergoing minor repair or fitting-out work. During construction, the decision was made to change this to a production facility. Bombing raids slowed construction, which was not completed until October 1944. Work on this bunker was shared by a number of contractors including Wayss & Freytag AG, Habermann & Guckes AG, Holzverartbeitung GmbH and G. Tesch of Berlin.

The bunker was just over 162m in length, 35m in width and 13m in height. It was used to facilitate the construction of *Seehund* mini-submarines and also modular sections of the Type XXI. Subsequent bombing raids after the completion of the facility did little damage and the bunker survived the war intact.

# Bremen

### Hornisse

Built on the north bank of the River Weser at Bremen, this complex was commissioned in early 1944. It was basically a sheltered construction complex which would be used (together with the much bigger Valentin bunker) to build the revolutionary Type XXI U-Boat. The Type XXI's design integrated modular sections so that the construction work could be distributed to suitable sites throughout Germany, sometimes far inland, then transported to assembly points at various shipyards for completion, launch and fitting out. A Type XXI could be built in about 176 days, about half the time it took to put together a Type VII or Type IX. The bunker was to be erected on land belonging to the Deschimar firm in Bremen on which an assembly yard had already been established. The bunker would simply protect this facility with a reinforced-concrete shell. The construction contract was awarded to the Hamburg firm of Wayss & Freytag.

In the eastern end of the bunker, which lay on a virtual east–west axis, an assembly line for the production of sectional modules was planned, whilst the centre section of the complex was to consist of two dry-dock pens for repair work. These pens would be connected to the westernmost section that consisted of two wet pens (but capable of being pumped out for dry-dock work) each capable of housing two Type XXIs. The pen areas were connected to each other, and to the exterior, by lock gates.

A heavy bombing raid by the USAAF on 30 March 1945 destroyed much of the construction, which was never completed.

### Valentin

Plans were first made in 1943 for the erection of a protected assembly facility on the banks of the River Weser at Farge near Bremen. This was to be a custom-built facility for the assembly of the Type XXI U-Boat (see above). One of the principal reasons why this excellent submarine could not be brought into service soon enough to influence the war at sea was the interruption to the building programme caused by Allied air raids – hence the decision to build this massive, reinforced-concrete protected facility. The facility was a virtual assembly line: the partially assembled boats moved through various stages until, finally finished, they were lowered into a wet pen and sailed out into the River Weser from the bunker.

The Type XXI consisted of eight hull sections, numbered from stern to bow, plus the conning tower. Main assembly points for this submarine were at the Blohm & Voss yard at Hamburg, Schichau in Danzig and at Deschimar AG Weser in Bremen, with Blohm & Voss producing the greatest number. As soon as the Allies became aware that this revolutionary new boat was being assembled at Blohm & Voss, the yard came under persistent attack by Allied bombers and suffered serious damage. Valentin, had it reached completion, would have been a valuable asset.

The interior of the unfinished Valentin bunker in May 1945. To the right is the wet basin into which the completed Type XXI boat would be lowered.

Over 12,000 workers were employed in the construction of this gigantic bunker, of which around one third were foreign, and over 2,500 were either prisoner-of-war forced labourers or concentration camp inmates. It is estimated that at least 4,000 died during the construction work on this bunker. Work ceased on 7 April 1945, at which point the bunker was around 90 per cent complete.

Allied bombing raids in late March 1945 succeeded in penetrating the partially completed structure with Tallboy bombs, but little damage was caused to the interior. There were only two major air raids, one on 27 March 1945 by the USAAF and one on 30 March by the RAF. The latter saw 15 Tallboys dropped, of which six were direct hits.

# Bergen

### Bruno

Shortly after the invasion of Norway in 1940, the Germans established naval bases at several ports, Bergen being one of the most important. In May 1942 work commenced on the construction of a U-Boat bunker at the Norwegian port. The bunker was built on a rocky outcrop in a small bay to the west of the town.

The bunker was planned to consist of ten pens, three of which would be wet and six dry. The tenth would be used for fuel storage. In the event, just seven pens were constructed: one of these was used for fuel storage, and of the remaining six, three were wet and three dry. The roof was up to 6m thick in places and the walls up to 4m thick. A further mezzanine level was built above the main bunker to provide additional storage space. This also had the beneficial effect of enhancing the level of protection against air attack for the bunker interior. The overall size of the Bruno bunker was 130m by 143m.

Unusually for such construction projects outside Germany, responsibility was not in the hands of the Organisation Todt. Instead a commercial construction firm, Wayss & Freytag AG, which had also worked on similar projects within Germany, was the main contractor. Each of the three wet pens, on the north side of the bunker, was 11m wide, and the dry pens 17m wide. Their entrances were protected by 3cm-thick steel doors formed by hanging, overlapping plates.

The base was to be the home of 11 Unterseebootsflotille for most of the war and following the Allied invasion of Normandy took on an even greater strategic importance as the French bases were, one by one, closed down and abandoned.

Work to enlarge and improve the bunker continued throughout the war. As the importance of the Bergen U-Boat base grew, so did the Allied determination to destroy it. The first major bombing raid, comprising over 130 RAF bombers, took place on 4 October 1944. Although the RAF raid caused widespread destruction to the surrounding area and serious civilian casualties, its effect on the bunkers was minimal. Direct hits were achieved, but none succeeded in penetrating the thick, reinforced-concrete shell.

RIGHT **Bruno bunker, Bergen, Norway**
The Bruno bunker at Bergen was originally intended to comprise a total of ten pens but in the event only seven were constructed. Of these, six (**A**–**F**) were used to accommodate U-Boats, whilst the seventh (**G**) was used for fuel storage. The complex covered an area of around 18,600m² and was protected by a roof almost 4m thick. On the roof, a number of storerooms were built and even a cafeteria. The floor to this mezzanine level added an additional 1.35m to the overall thickness of the roof, increasing protection for the boats inside. Although entrances to the three dry-dock pens (**D**, **E** and **F**) were protected by vertical, overlapping steel plates, the wet pens (**A**, **B** and **C**) were open to the harbour.

|   | **Ground floor** | **First floor** |
|---|---|---|
| 1 | Gunnery workshop | Signals workshop |
| 2 | Ship repair workshop | Periscope repair workshop |
| 3 | Blacksmith and welding shop | Ship repair workshop |
| 4 | Mechanical workshop | Engineering workshop |
| 5 | Torpedo store | Engineering workshop |
| 6 | Torpedo store | Electrical workshop |
| 7 | Battery store | |
| 8 | Emergency generator | |
| 9 | *Treibol-Schmierollager* pump room | |

39

A further attack on 29 October saw almost 250 RAF aircraft involved, though less than 50 eventually found and bombed the target. Not one German casualty was inflicted though once again there was considerable loss of civilian life. No damage was suffered by the bunker interior, all of the blast effect being dissipated in the space between the outer and inner roof levels.

A third and final raid on 12 January 1945 was launched by 32 RAF bombers carrying Tallboy bombs. The bunkers at Bergen survived the war intact.

## Trondheim

### Dora I

The U-Boat bunker at Trondheim was the first to be constructed in Norway. It was a relatively small structure, measuring some 153m in length and 111m in width, with just five pens. Of these, three were 15m in width, had dry-dock capabilities and could accommodate just one boat each: two were 21m-wide wet pens, each of these could accommodate two boats. The main purpose of the bunker was to provide repair facilities for 13 Unterseebootsflotille. Air raid protection was provided by three 2cm flak installations on the bunker roof.

As with most bunkers outside Germany, construction was overseen by the Organisation Todt, and specifically by the OT-Einstazgruppe Wiking. The principal contractor was the Munich firm of Sager & Wörner. Orders for construction of the bunker were issued at the start of 1941 and it took fully 27 months to complete the work. Several thousand workers were involved, including around 800 Soviet prisoners of war used as forced labour.

Only one major air raid, on 24 July 1943, was suffered by the Dora I bunker: a subsequent raid launched on 22 November 1944, comprising over 170 RAF bombers, was abandoned due to poor visibility over the target area. Dora I survived the war intact.

### Dora II

Almost as soon as work on Dora I had commenced, it was realised that a greater capacity would be required and planning began for a new bunker (Dora II) in the same harbour and just 140m away. Dora II was to have four additional pens, two 13.5m-wide wet and two 20m-wide dry, thus allowing for the accommodation of a further six boats.

Immediately behind the dry pens was the boiler room, and behind the wet pens a storage space. Running the full width of the bunker behind these would be all of the electrical gear for the bunker, and further to the rear, workshops for repairing the boats' battery cells, and torpedo storage areas.

Unfortunately, the demand for skilled workers by the huge bunkers being constructed in France meant that the small workforce available for the second bunker at Trondheim made slow progress, and the structure was only 60 per

BELOW LEFT The Dora I bunker in May 1945. Tied up alongside the quay are *U-861* and *U-995*.

BELOW RIGHT The interior of the U-Boat bunker at Trondheim. Note the corrugated metal shuttering on the ceiling. As shown here, most of the wet pens were capable of accommodating two boats.

cent complete when the war ended. A third bunker, Dora III, was also planned at Leangen, just to the east of Trondheim, but the project was cancelled before any serious construction work had been done.

# Brest

Almost as soon as construction work on the pens began in January 1941 (see 'Tour of a U-Boat base' for details), the site was subjected to Allied air raids. In the spring of 1943, work began on strengthening the roof of the bunker. Ultimately the roof had a thickness in excess of 6m, and a layer of concrete beams was laid across the roof some 3.8m above its surface (the *Fangrost* concept): these beams were around 1.5m high and spaced about the same distance apart.

Continued air raids caused very little damage to the bunkers and cost the Allies dearly in lost aircraft. Air defence for the bunker itself was provided by three 4cm flak guns in concrete emplacements and controlled by their own radar equipment.

Eventually, however, a series of Tallboy raids in early August 1944 was launched against the Brest U-Boat bunkers. A total of nine direct hits were scored from 26 bombs dropped. Of these five actually penetrated the roof, but caused little or no damage to the interior and none whatsoever to the U-Boats inside.

Throughout the war the U-Boat bunker at Brest suffered more enemy air raids than any other base. Over 80 large-scale raids were launched between 1941 and 1945, and of these 11 were the so-called 'hundred-bomber raids' with up to 154 aircraft taking part. Around 50 aircraft were either shot down in these raids, or so badly damaged that they were destroyed on landing.

The rapid progress being made by Allied troops following the Normandy landings in June 1944 saw the U-Boat bunker at Brest under serious threat. The last U-Boat to depart from the bunker was *U-256*, under the command of Korvettenkapitän Heinrich Lehmann-Willenbrock, which left on 4 September. Lehmann-Willenbrock was the real-life commander of *U-96*, upon which the fictional film *Das Boot* was based.

US forces finally captured the port on 21 September 1944 after four weeks of extremely bitter fighting. The US Army suffered over 10,000 casualties in this battle by the end of which the port itself had been almost totally destroyed – except for the U-Boat bunker, which remained intact.

# Lorient

The port of Lorient fell to the German Army on 21 June 1940, and just 16 days later the first U-Boat (*U-30* under Kapitänleutnant Fritz-Julius Lemp) docked at the port for resupply. Lorient soon became one of the Kriegsmarine's most vital U-Boat bases. The base eventually housed two flotillas, 2 Unterseebootsflotille 'Salzwedel' and 10 Unterseebootsflotille.

The first facility provided for U-Boats was a winching system for pulling smaller vessels out of the water for inspection and repair. This was based around a smaller pre-existing facility for fishing boats on the Keroman peninsula, which was upgraded and enlarged. Here fishing boats were winched up a ramp onto a turntable, which could then direct them onto one of six sets of stocks. Due to both the limited capacity of the winching mechanisms and the size of the bunkers, these were used only for smaller U-Boats.

The next major improvement was the building of the two so-called *Dombunker* or 'cathedral bunkers', also at Keroman: they acquired their name because of their high, arched roofs. These small bunkers were built at the fishing-boat repair facility, immediately to the east of the main complex, over the two southernmost positions. Built by the firm of Carl Brand of Düren, each bunker was 81m long, 16m wide and 25m high and had walls some 1.5m thick. U-Boats could be winched on trolleys directly from the water and along into these dry bunkers. They were nowhere near as well protected as the main

Here we see the so-called 'cathedral' (*Dom*) bunkers built to accommodate the small Type II U-Boats at the old fishing-boat repair yard at Lorient.

Another of Lorient's interesting structures was the turntable fitting at the top of the old fishing-boat repair ramp. This was strengthened and improved to handle small Type II coastal U-Boats. Here a Type II, partially covered by tarpaulins, has been winched up out of the water and into one of the repair areas. However, these boats were dangerously exposed to enemy attack.

bunker complex: they were intended to provide U-Boats undergoing repair and maintenance some measure of protection from shrapnel and the like. They were strong, but would not have been able to withstand a direct hit from a Tallboy as the main bunkers did on several occasions.

In April 1941, a more conventional-style U-Boat bunker was also built further up the River Scorff, on the eastern bank across from the existing port dry-dock facilities. Known as the 'Scorff bunker' for obvious reasons, this structure consisted of two pens just over 100m long with workshop and repair facilities to the rear of the structure. The overall length of the bunker was 128m.

Surveyors meantime had been searching for a suitable location for the creation of a larger bunker complex. Once again the Keroman peninsula was chosen, and an area extending to around 50 acres was taken over by the Kriegsmarine. Work on the first bunker, subsequently known as Keroman I, began in 1941 with over 15,000 workers being employed in construction.

A rather ingenious design was created for this particular complex. The bunker consisted of a well-protected, enclosed wet bunker with five pens. On the east side of the bunker was an enclosed berth, the floor of which was sloped. Sitting on this ramp was a 45m-long cradle into which the boat sailed. The water in this berth would then be pumped out, effectively lowering the boat into the cradle which sat on a wheeled trolley, with the aid of an overhead crane. The trolley was then winched up a 160m sloped slipway: at the top, the cradle was moved from the trolley onto a similarly designed 48m-long traversing unit. This unit moved backwards and forwards along eight sets of rails, running between the two sets of five dry pens, allowing it to be brought perfectly in line with any of the individual pens. The trolley unit was then run off the traverser into the selected pen. The operation to move the submarine from Keroman I across exposed open space into the safe bunkers of Keroman II took between one and two hours from start to finish. The unique equipment was manufactured by the M.A.N. (Maschinenfabrik Augsburg-Nürnberg) firm, and this amazing system was so well built that it is still fully functional today.

The pens in Keroman I were 120m long, 85m wide and 18.5m in height, with 2.4m-thick walls and a roof over 3m thick. Each pen was provided with a travelling crane. Keroman I was completed in September 1941. At the same time, work was under way on a further bunker complex, known as Keroman II, directly in line with the existing complex at the top of the slope. This contained a further seven dry pens, each 138m long, 120m wide and 18.5m in height. Each pen in Keroman II was provided with two travelling cranes. An eighth pen was also built but this contained the equipment for the traversing unit.

A third bunker, Keroman III, was begun in October 1941 and completed in January 1943. This provided a further seven pens, all opening out directly into deep water and capable of being used for both wet and dry docking. The pens were 170m long, 135m wide and 20m in height and each was provided with a travelling crane. The concrete roof was over 7m thick.

A further bunker complex, Keroman IV, was planned to provide facilities for the new Type XXI submarines, but due to Germany's wartime reversals, this project was not carried through.

In addition to the bunker complex proper, the entire Lorient base was liberally peppered with smaller bunkers, including a complex of six torpedo storage bunkers to the north-west of the Keroman complex, linked to the base by a narrow-gauge track. The Lorient base was also heavily defended by a huge range of anti-aircraft artillery ranging from light 2cm flak guns, of which there were over 200, through medium 7.5cm and 8.8cm pieces, up to heavy 10.5cm and 12.8cm flak guns.

The bunker complexes at Lorient were bombed on numerous occasions but no serious damage was ever inflicted. A total of 33 significant air raids on the bunkers were recorded, though only one of these, on 17 May 1943, involved over 100 aircraft. At least 60 enemy aircraft were either shot down or seriously damaged during these raids. Additional protection against low-level attack by enemy aircraft was provided by mooring two elderly ships directly in front of the bunkers: they had particularly tall masts and barrage balloons tethered to their superstructure. Despite the Allied advances through France, the German garrison at Lorient held out right until the end of the war. The last U-Boat to leave, *U-155*, departed on 5 September 1944, with two other boats, the severely damaged *U-123* and *U-129*, left behind. The port finally surrendered to US Army troops on 10 May 1945, two days after VE-Day.

This photo shows a Type IX U-Boat being winched up in its special cradle onto dry land from the docking pen at Keroman I at Lorient. This pen was not a working area as such, and therefore had only a very narrow walkway along one side.

## St Nazaire

The port of St Nazaire fell to the Germans in the summer of 1940. Work on constructing the U-Boat bunkers began in March 1941 in the southern basin of the harbour. The first four of an eventual total of 14 pens were ready for use by July 1941 whilst work continued on the remainder of the structure. The first five pens were some 130m long and 18m high. Each was 14m wide with a dividing wall between each pen 1.25m to 1.5m thick. Separating Pen 1 from the north-side exterior was a 22m-wide storage space area, running the full length of the pen. Between pens 5 and 6 was a storage area running the length of the pen and some 8m wide. Pens 6 to 8 were identical to the first five. Then followed pens 9 to 12, shorter than the previous pens at just 124m in length, but wider at 20m and separated by dividing walls 1.25m thick. A further spaced area some 8m wide separated Pen 12 from pens 13 and 14 which once again were 20m wide.

To the rear of the bunker complex, immediately behind each pen, were a number of workshop areas, each the same width as the pen. On the north and south side walls of the complex, in line with the rear of the pens, was a 5m-wide entrance door leading to a corridor running the full width of the complex. Overall the bunker complex was 295m wide. Six of the pens were wet whilst the others were capable of being pumped out and used for dry-docking. Its first resident U-Boat flotilla, Unterseebootsflotille 7 'Wegener', arrived in June 1941. In February 1942, the Wegener flotilla was joined at St Nazaire by Unterseebootsflotille 6 'Hundius'.

In mid-1943 the Organisation Todt began work on reinforcing the bunker roof, adding almost 4m to its thickness. Originally, U-Boats had to first enter the main (north) basin via the Normandie dock, and then pass through a smaller lock into the southern basin. The British commando attack in March 1942, when the explosive-laden destroyer HMS *Campbeltown* was rammed into the gate of the dock and detonated, highlighted the vulnerability of the system. Accordingly, a new lock was built directly opposite the entrance to the bunkers, giving direct access to open water and protected by a concrete bunker.

The boat is now almost fully within the receiving pen. Although the ceiling of the pen is extremely high, the conning tower of the submarine will only just clear the entrance to the pen.

The bunkers proved themselves during numerous Allied air raids, with no loss or damage suffered by any U-Boat inside – despite the almost total destruction of the town. In all, 30 major raids were recorded on the St Nazaire bunkers, three in particular being extremely heavy. On 28 February 1943, over 430 RAF bombers pounded the port. This was followed on 22 March by another raid involving over 350 aircraft, and one on 28 March of over 320 aircraft. A total of 58 enemy aircraft are recorded as having been lost during these raids.

A view from inside the pen, with the boat now fully in. Note the rails along which its trolley has been wheeled, and the considerable height of the U-Boat's deck above the ground.

## Keroman I, II and III, Lorient

The largest and most impressive of all complexes was the one at Lorient. This illustration shows the entire complex. At the former fishing-boat repair site (**1**) boats would be pulled up the ramp by winch onto the central turntable unit (**2**), which would then rotate to send the boat on its cradle towards one of the '*Dom*' bunkers shown around the central turntable (**3** and **4**). At bottom right is the Keroman III bunker (**A**), a large unit with seven pens opening out into the River Le Ter. In the lower left of the illustration is the original Keroman I bunker (**B**): note the pen opening into the Le Ter (**5**). This entrance led to the ramp (**6**) that gave access to the upper-level Keroman II bunker (**C**), protected by a lock gate. The pen interior would be drained and the boat lowered by an overhead crane onto a special cradle on a wheeled trolle. It would then be winched up the 160m-long slope and onto the traversing unit (**7**) running between Keroman I and Keroman II. This unit was 48m long and 13m wide and ran along an eight-rail track. In addition to the entrance pen, Keroman I (**B**) had a total of five dry repair pens. Directly opposite, in Keroman II (**C**), there were a further seven repair pens. The traversing unit allowed the boat to be lined up with any of the repair pens and winched along a four-rail track into the appropriate pen. It would normally take around two hours for a boat to be taken out of the water, winched up the slope and received into one of the repair pens. The traverser units themselves were stored in a separate pen alongside Keroman II (**8**). An extension to Keroman II (Keroman IVb) and an extension to Keroman I (Keroman IVa) are shown under construction (**9**), though neither was ever completed: the resources were channelled into the construction of Keroman III instead.

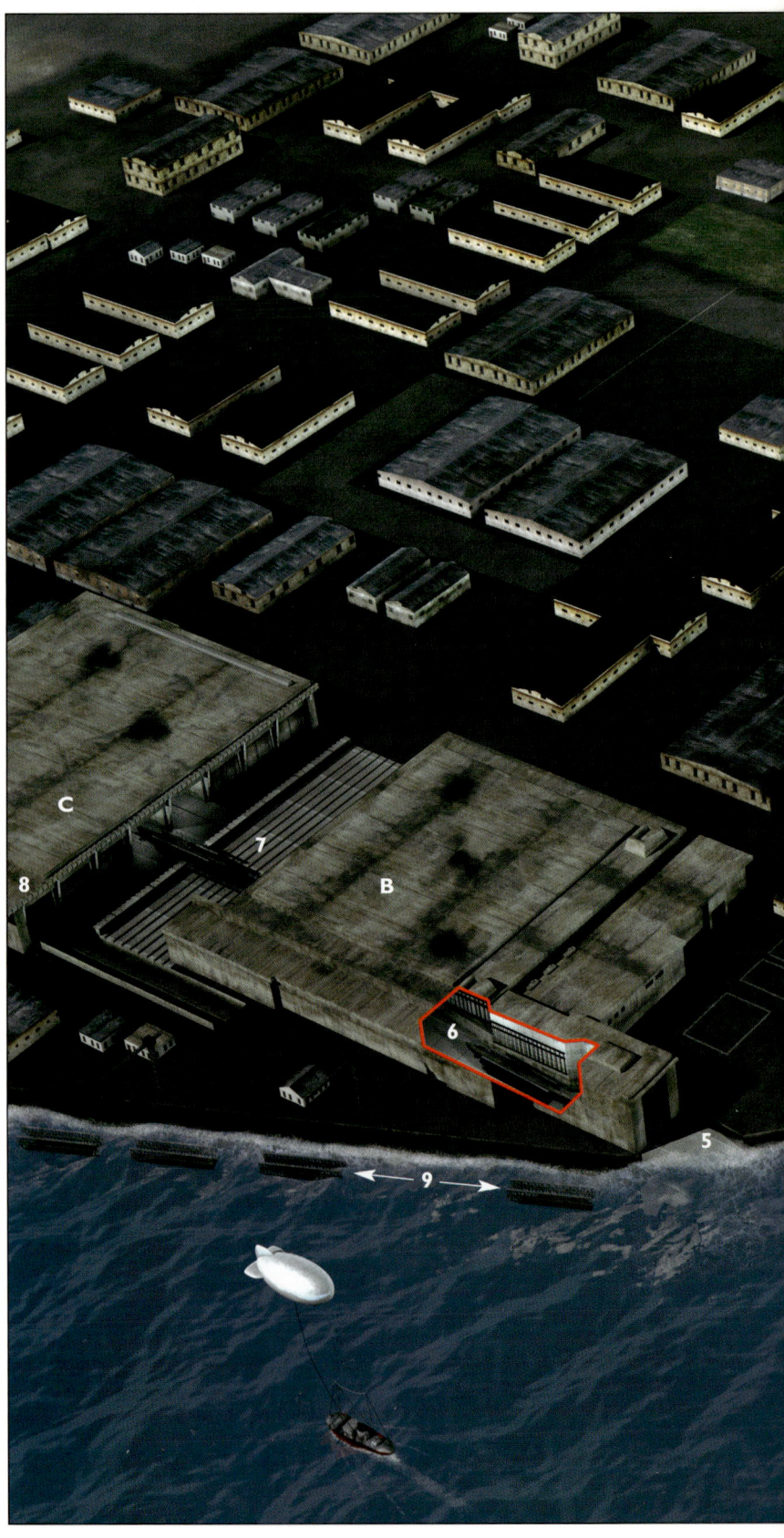

This view clearly shows the Lorient traversing unit sitting on its set of eight parallel rails. Note that the protective steel doors on two of the pens have been closed, suggesting that perhaps U-Boats are inside undergoing repairs or maintenance work.

Following D-Day, the U-Boats based at St Nazaire were withdrawn to Norway, the last of this batch (*U-267*) departing on 23 September 1944. The base, though, was rigorously defended, having been declared by Hitler to be a 'fortress'. Troops under the command of Generalleutnant Junck resisted all Allied attempts to take the port until the very last day of the war. During this period however, numerous U-Boats made the trip to St Nazaire carrying essential supplies: as late as February 1945, *U-275* docked for repairs to its schnorkel equipment. The very last boat to leave was *U-255*, which had been languishing at St Nazaire for some time awaiting repairs. Following the arrival in the autumn of 1944 of a seaplane carrying spare parts, repair work was carried out and *U-255* eventually left St Nazaire on 8 May 1945, just in time to surrender to the Allies.

The last boat to put in to St Nazaire was *U-510*, which arrived at the end of a long voyage from the Far East on 23 April 1945. She was still there when the Allies finally took over the port, and was in such good order that she was taken into the French Navy where she served as the *Bouan*.

## La Pallice

This base, often erroneously referred to as La Rochelle, fell to the Germans in 1940, but did not become a major U-Boat operational base until the autumn of 1941. Initially, it was used by the submarines of the Italian Navy, but in the spring of 1941 it was decided that a new U-Boat base would be built on the eastern side of the main basin of this port. Construction of the bunker began in April 1941 and on 27 October of that year, following the completion of the first two pens, it became home to Unterseebootsflotille 3 Lohs. The first U-Boats arrived within three weeks.

Around 490 Organisation Todt personnel were involved in the construction of this bunker, overseeing 1,800 forced labourers. The bunker complex was to consist of ten pens. The first two to be completed were wet pens, 92.5m in length and 17m in width, allowing each to accommodate two boats. Pens 3 to 7 were dry-dock capable, also 92.5m in length but just 11m wide, each capable of accommodating a single boat. Pens 8 and 9 were also dry-dock capable but slightly longer at 100m. Pen 10, also intended to function as a dry dock, was never fully completed. It was to be 17m wide and capable of accommodating two boats.

The quays separating each pen were between 4.25m and 5m wide with a dividing wall running down the centre of each. The exception to this was the

An operational Type VIIC U-Boat enters the bunker at La Pallice. Note the disruptive-pattern camouflage painted on the bunker structure.

space between pens 7 and 8, which consisted of a 15m-wide quay running all the way through the bunker complex and extending out into the basin as a 200m-long mole. This mole also carried twin railway lines.

Overall, the complex measured 195m by 165m and was 14m high. The roof thickness over pens 1 to 5 was in excess of 7m. Work was still ongoing to increase the existing 6.5m-thick roof over the remaining pens and to install bomb traps when the worsening war situation brought this to a halt. On the exterior, at the north-eastern corner of the rear of the bunker, was a 30m-wide and 50m-long concrete structure, some 25m high: this contained a generating station for the bunker. Against the southern side wall of the bunker by the side entrance door was an oil storage bunker.

The bunker suffered much less from the attentions of enemy bombers than some of its counterparts, only eight major raids being launched against it, none of which did any serious damage to the pens. Anti-aircraft defences on the bunker complex consisted of three concrete emplacements for 2cm light flak guns. In addition to the U-Boat bunker complex, numerous other subsidiary bunkers were constructed, including three large torpedo storage bunkers around a kilometre to the north-east of the U-Boat bunker complex. A command bunker and a small bunker housing the electricity transformer were located to the west of these storage bunkers. Also, a large bunker-type construction was built over the lock that allowed entrance into the basin where the U-Boat bunker complex was located.

As with the other French bases, its usefulness decreased after 6 June 1944 and its boats were dispersed to other bases, primarily in Norway. This base, too, was declared a 'fortress' and its garrison held out until 8 May 1945. A Type VIIC U-Boat (*U-766*) was still in residence when the base finally surrendered, and was taken into the French Navy as the *Laubie*.

## Bordeaux

The port at Bordeaux became an operational Axis naval base in the autumn of 1940 when it became home to the Italian Navy's submarine flotilla Betasom, whose operational success was, it must be said, somewhat limited. Admiral Dönitz decided in mid-1941 to erect a protective U-Boat bunker in the port's Number 2 basin, entered first through a lock from the River Gironde into the Number 1 basin, then through a further lock between the two.

The U-Boat bunker comprised 11 pens. Pens 1 to 4 were wet pens 105m long and 20m wide, capable of accommodating two boats each. Pens 5 to 8 were also 105m long, but just 14m wide, designed to accommodate one boat each. Pens 9

to 11 were dry-dock capable, and were 95m long and 11m wide. Overall, the complex was 245m wide, 162m long, and 19m high, with roofing just under 6m thick. At the north-east corner of the structure was a 58m-wide and 73m-long concrete blockhouse containing the bunker boiler room and electrical equipment.

This base primarily served the larger Type IX boats used for long-distance cruises, as well as the Type XIV 'Milk Cows' and the Type XB minelayers. Bordeaux became the home base for 12 Unterseebootsflotille, which also took over the remaining Italian submarines after Italy's surrender. All but one of these Italian submarines sailed from Bordeaux to the Far East on transport missions, some eventually being taken over by the Imperial Japanese Navy – thus having served three different masters.

Earlier in the war, Bordeaux was also visited by Japanese submarines, which successfully made the long journey from Japan to occupied Europe. As with all the French bases, Bordeaux came under attack by Allied bombers. However, the port suffered only seven major air raids from 1940 through to mid-1944: two larger bombing raids in August 1944 saw the bunkers suffer little or no serious damage. The base was finally abandoned in late-August 1944 and was occupied by Free French Forces on the 26th of that month, the last few U-Boats having put to sea just two days earlier.

# After the war – the fate of the bases

## Hamburg

At the end of the war, the Elbe II bunker fell into British hands intact. On 11 November 1945, British troops from the Royal Engineers blew up the bunker, using a stock of captured German Luftwaffe bombs: this caused the central dividing wall between the two bunkers to collapse, and without this support, the roof partially caved in. Three Type XXI boats, *U-2505*, *U-3004* and *U-3506*, were still inside. The demolition work resulted in the roof totally crushing *U-3506* when it came down, though the other two remained reasonably intact.

In 1949 the first salvage work on the U-Boats inside the bunker began. The boats were pumped dry and internal components such as the precious accumulator cells, copper cabling, and some diesel engines, were removed from the wrecks of the Type XXIs. *U-2501*, which had been sunk right at the entrance to the bunker in May 1945, was raised and scrapped during the 1950s: further operations saw the stern sections of *U-2505* and *U-3004* blown off to allow further materials to be salvaged. At this point work stopped due to the unsafe nature of the bunker. The Type XXIs were left largely undisturbed for several decades – apart from the attention of souvenir hunters who discovered that access to the bunker was still possible, and would descend on the boats when they were briefly exposed at low tide.

In the early 1960s, some attempts were made to clear the site and a substantial quantity of reinforced concrete was removed before escalating costs forced a halt to the project. No further attempts were made to complete the demolition, a decision in which the sheer cost of such an operation played a major role.

A decision was finally made in 1995 to infill the pens, partly due to the fact that they were still accessible and clearly in a dangerous state. It was feared that lives would be lost as it was proving impossible to keep souvenir hunters away. It was by now completely out of the question that the bunker might be demolished, as estimated costs had risen to a staggering DM 300,000,000. By 8 October 1995, the remains of the two Type XXIs had been buried under countless tons of sand.

The exterior of the Elbe II bunker. The interior walls were blown out and the roof collapsed: its massive sloping slabs are clearly visible leaning against the top of the remaining wall.

Until recently, the remains of the Elbe II bunker were still accessible, including the rusting hulks of Type XXI U-Boats left inside when the bunker was demolished. As the tide receded the hulls would be exposed. The bows of one submarine can just been seen in the gloomy interior, running from upper left to lower right. The bunker was considered too dangerous to be left in such a condition, and so was infilled with sand. The boats inside are now buried.

No further efforts to clear the partly demolished remains seem to have been made yet. Officially, there is no access to the area today but there is little or nothing to prevent a visit to the site. The bunker remains lie within the port of Hamburg, on the south bank of the River Elbe which runs through the city, just by the Vulcanhafen yard.

In October 1945, the intact Fink II bunker was used by the Royal Engineers to effectively kill two birds with one stone. The bunker was filled with over 30 tons of unexploded German bombs from Luftwaffe stores that had fallen into British hands and needed to be safely disposed of. The detonation of this ordnance rid the British of this dangerous material and also caused the collapse of the bunker, bringing down the roof and shattering the walls. Further demolition work was carried out after the City of Hamburg authorised the clearance of the site in 1949. One of the firms contracted to remove the remains of the bunker was, ironically, Dyckerhoff & Widmann AG, one of the main contractors for erecting the bunkers during the war years.

By the 1970s, the famed Deutsche Werft firm, on whose land the bunker stood, had succumbed to the general world recession. The whole site, including the bunker area was cleared, with only a few small buildings remaining, all traces of Fink II having been removed. The area was grassed over and is now a recreation facility open to the public.

## Kiel

Demolition work on the Kilian bunker in Kiel began in September 1945 when troops from the Royal Engineers began preparations for dynamiting the structure. Several weeks were spent drilling hundreds of holes into the concrete structure, and packing them with explosives. As with the Fink II bunker, a quantity of unused Luftwaffe bombs were also packed into the exterior. The resultant explosion collapsed the dividing wall between the two pens and brought down the roof, crushing the remains of the Type XXI boat *U-4708* still inside. The ruins were left in this state until 1959 when further clearance work was carried out by a German civil contractor. There still remains, however, considerable visible evidence of the bunker's presence. Although the roof and walls are gone and most of the pen area has been infilled and generally used as a dumping ground, at low tide the remains of the lower parts of the walls can be seen and part of the rear workshop area has been left standing. The vertical pillars of the entrance to the southernmost pen are still visible, as is the pier

ABOVE The after-effects of the Kilian bunker explosion. Most of the bunker has been destroyed.

LEFT The remains of the Hornisse bunker. There is little indication of its former purpose, and the bunker roof now supports a modern office block.

that separated the two pens, though this is now heavily overgrown. Since the late 1990s the Kilian remains have been open to the public, with guided tours available by special arrangement.

The other bunker at Kiel, Konrad, was blown up by the Royal Engineers in 1946, with much of the remains left in situ until the 1960s. At that point the remains were cleared to make way for the expansion of the Howaldtswerke shipyard. No trace of the bunker structure remains, and the area where it was situated is now open land.

## Bremen

The massive Valentin complex at Bremen was used after the war for bombing practice by both the RAF and USAAF. Some bomb penetration of this incomplete bunker had been achieved in March 1945, though the structure remained mostly intact. For some reason, unlike the other German bunkers, the British made no attempt to demolish this structure. Perhaps its sheer size and the potential cost of

RIGHT **Type XXI U-Boats under construction at Valentin, Bremen**

This illustration shows how the Valentin bunker, a superbly protected construction facility, was intended to function. The Type XXI was assembled from pre-fabricated sections, the manufacture of which was subcontracted to various firms throughout Germany. These sections could be brought into the complex overland or up river by barge, and into the bunker via the opening into the River Weser.

The 13-stage assembly process would have begun in the south-west corner of the complex (**A**), where stages one to three would see the keel being laid and the partially completed hull modules welded together. Moving on 30-ton trolleys, each unit would be shifted northwards right to the opposite end of the bunker, where it would then be traversed into the central section (**B**) and moved back along the bunker. Here, during stages four to eight, the welding work would be completed, machinery installed, the tanks tested and the conning tower added.

On reaching the far end of the bunker, the boat would undergo stages nine and ten where its batteries, periscopes and schnorkel tube would be fitted: the periscopes were lowered into place using a five-ton overhead crane (**C**). The roof of the bunker was higher at this point to allow for the extreme length of the periscope. The boat then reversed direction again, and moved towards the bunker exit. Through stages 11 and 12 the final fitting out was done, the antennae installed. Then (stage 13) the boat moved sideways into the flooded end chamber and into water some 9m deep, where it was

tested to ensure it was watertight and fuel and oil taken on. The completed boat would then be moved out into the River Weser. The seaward entrance/exit was protected by lock gates. The rear area (**D**), as in most bunkers, was given over to workshops, stores and similar units.

There were four levels in the Valentin complex. At ground level were the boiler house, assembly and mechanical workshops, toolmakers' workshop, a smithy and heat-treating workshop, a first-aid room and toilets. A mezzanine floor was intended to accommodate an administrative area with various offices for quality control, provisions, medical supplies, accounts, a tool store, a despatch office and further toilet facilities. Among the facilities planned for the first floor were a battery storeroom, a plumbers' workshop, carpenters' shop, timber store, electrical workshop, metalworking shop and sheet metal store. At roof level more office accommodation was planned, including offices for the various managers of construction, personnel, business managers, accounts as well as radio operators and telegraphists. There were also stores for sheet metal, piping, wire, screws and other standard components plus oil storage.

The first orders for Valentin-produced Type XXI U-Boats were placed in May 1944, with the first boats scheduled to be completed in October of that year. Delays in construction of the complex saw the first estimated launch put back until April 1945 – but the war ended before any boats could be produced at this facility. The current German Navy still uses the various storage and office areas at the rear of the bunker.

ABOVE The western face of the Valentin bunker. On the left is the entrance through which component sub-assemblies could be brought by barge and through which the completed Type XXI would exit into the River Weser. Since the end of the war, the entrance has been blocked off and the embankment built up alongside this west face. Although the opening is closed off by a wire-mesh screen, it is still possible to see into the interior of the complex.

such an operation were influential. In the autumn of 1964, the bunker was once again taken over by the German Armed Forces and is still in use as a storage depot for the Bundesmarine (access to the interior is therefore not possible).

The Valentin bunker still stands today relatively intact, and this massive edifice is well worth a visit. It can be accessed by public road via the village of Farge, some 25km downstream from Bremen on the banks of the River Weser. Near the front entrance is a memorial to the forced labourers who lost their lives during the construction of this colossus. A public footpath runs along the south face of the bunker beside the banks of the Weser, and visitors can look into the exit which was to have allowed the Type XXI U-Boats to sail out of the bunker and into the river. Although this final launch pen is still filled with water, there is no longer any direct route from the pen to the river, the bank having been built up and the channel leading to the Weser filled in.

## Helgoland

The U-Boat bunkers on Helgoland were still relatively intact at the end of the war, many of the other defensive structures (gun emplacements and the like). Many were destroyed or seriously damaged, although a number of powerful weapons still remained operable though. On the cessation of hostilities, over 4,500 German personnel, including over 1,100 civilian workers, were still on the fortress island. Most military personnel were then evacuated to the mainland, leaving only a small handover party, which formally surrendered the Helgoland fortifications to Admiral Gould of the Royal Navy on 11 May 1945.

Following the decision of the occupying powers to demilitarise Germany, in August 1945 a special force of demolition workers, mostly German and under the command of a Royal Navy officer, began work on preparing for the demolition of all surviving structures, including the U-Boat bunkers. Thousands of tons of explosives were shipped to the island and added to the vast amounts of

The south wall of the Valentin bunker, showing the side entrance through which component sub-assemblies could be brought into the facility.

unused ammunition already on site. The surviving bunkers were packed full of ammunition and explosives.

On 18 April 1947, preparations were completed and all personnel withdrawn from the island. From a British warship lying some nine miles offshore, the explosives were detonated. The resultant explosion went into the record books as the largest man-made non-atomic explosion in history. The U-Boat bunkers were totally destroyed. Little remains, although one tower has been converted into a lighthouse.

# Bergen

Shortly after the end of the war, troops of the Royal Engineers demolished a large part of the Bergen U-Boat bunker complex. In 1949, however, the Royal Norwegian Navy repaired and refitted the dry-dock facilities and at the same time infilled pens 4, 5 and 6, forming a quay alongside the dry-dock facilities. These, along with the workshop part of the bunker, are still in use by the Norwegian Navy today, so access to the interior is not possible.

# Trondheim

As with the complex at Bergen, a large part of the Trondheim bunker Dora II was demolished by the Royal Engineers at the end of the war. Only a small portion (the workshop area) remains and is used by a civilian boat-building and repair firm for storage. Dora I, however, survived intact and was taken over by the Royal Norwegian Navy, continuing its original function as a submarine bunker. In 1955 it was decommissioned and handed over for civilian use as a storage facility: a car park was built on the roof of the bunker in 1988. The pens can be photographed from various vantage points around the harbour.

# The French bases

The U-Boat bunkers at these bases fell into Allied hands in almost perfect condition with no significant damage from enemy attacks, with the exception of Brest. The following chapter contains details of the fate of the French bases following war's end, as well as information on how to get to the most accessible and best preserved sites in France. For a convenient starting point, travelling from the U.K. has been assumed. The nearest ferry port for a trip to the U-Boat bunkers would be Roscoff: the directions that follow are based upon travelling by road from there.

# Visiting U-Boat bases and bunkers today

## Brest

Following their capture by Allied forces at the end of the war, the U-Boat bunker at Brest were found to be basically intact. Some damage had been done, though none of it fatal to the structure. Lumps of concrete dislodged by bomb blasts had fallen into the water around the pens and the Germans, before surrendering, had sunk blocking ships in them to prevent their use by the enemy, as well as dumping considerable amounts of unexploded ordnance into the water. In time, all of this debris was removed and the pens brought back into use.

The U-Boat pens are still in use by the French Navy, and so cannot be accessed by the public. The area directly to the rear of the bunker complex is still accessible by public road (Route de la Corniche) and the almost perfect condition of the bunker makes this a worthwhile visit even if the interior itself cannot be seen.

From Roscoff, follow the signs for St Pol (D769), then on to the D58. Follow this road until the junction with the D10 and take the D788 exit. Follow the D788 until the junction with the D69 at the edge of Plouvorn. Following the signposts for Brest will bring you to the junction with the N12 which will take you all the way to this historic port.

## Bordeaux

The U-Boat bunkers at Bordeaux stand pretty much as they did in 1945. The bunkers are now in private hands and permission to visit them can be arranged. Be aware that maintenance work has not been carried out over the years: some parts of the bunker complex are now somewhat dangerous and entry is forbidden. A bus service runs from the main railway station in Bordeaux right to the banks of the Garonne, just a few minutes' walk from the bunker complex. A good view of the interior of the pens can be had from the quayside.

Once again, from the ferry port of Roscoff, follow the signs for St Pol (D769), then on to the D58: follow this until the junction with the D173, where you should bear right onto the D19. Follow this route until the junction with the

The Brest bunker today, put to much more peaceful use than during its service with the Kriegsmarine.

N12. A large portion of the journey, some 186km, is on this road: follow it until the junction with the N136. After 7.5km, follow the signposts for Nantes on the N137. Around 95 km further on, join the A844/N844/D844 until Junction 48 and join the A83 at Porte des Sorinieres. Follow this road for about 146km before changing on to the N148, following this briefly before joining the N11 and the N150 at the junction with the Niort Southern Bypass. Leave this road at the junction with the N248, and just over 2km later join the main A10/E5. This route takes the driver to within 5km of Bordeaux: leave the motorway at Junction 4 and travel along the N210 into the city.

The Bordeaux bunker complex today, still in remarkably good condition. The remains of the painted numbers above each pen are still visible.

## Lorient

The bunkers were taken over by the French Navy and continued to accommodate one of its original inhabitants, *U-123*, now known as *S-10 Blaison*. Keroman III is used as a dry-dock facility by nuclear submarines. Fortunately however, the French naval authorities appreciate the historical significance of this site and the public interest therein, and from the middle of June to the middle of September guided tours of the Keroman complex are available. It must be emphasised, however, that as this is still an active French Navy base: photography is strictly forbidden. Although access to the bunkers is not possible at other times, it is still possible to approach quite close to the bunker exteriors in many cases. The sensitivity to photography however must still be borne in mind.

The Keroman complex at Lorient today: this imposing structure is still in an excellent state of repair. Much of the complex was taken over by the French Navy, including the docking pen, winching ramp and traversing unit. The concrete anti-aircraft gun emplacements can be seen on the roof of the complex.

Both 'Dom' bunkers are still in existence, one having been abandoned and the other still in use by a civilian boat-building firm. These bunkers, being outside the naval base, may be approached without problem. The Scorff bunkers are now used to house surface vessels: access to these bunkers is prohibited. The former mansion at Kerneval, employed by Dönitz as headquarters of the Befehlshaber der U-Boote, is used by the French commanding admiral.

Follow the route given for Brest as far as the N12 junction, but turn off on to the D30 and follow this until meeting the D764. This route in turn should be followed to the junction with the D18. Follow the D18 until the junction signposted for Quimper, joining the N165 which can be followed all the way to the outskirts of Lorient: the final 3km of the route are along the D29.

## St Nazaire

The St Nazaire complex fell into Allied hands intact with one of its inhabitants in reasonably good order. After minor repairs, *U-510* served with the French Navy. The bunker has remained in use ever since, although having been abandoned as naval establishments the pens were allowed to silt up and some have even been infilled. The bunker complex at St Nazaire is in an entirely civilian area, and may thus be approached without problem. Notices point out that access is prohibited, although this is because it is still used by commercial firms for storage, as opposed to military use. It is believed that one of the pens may be cleared and used to house a decommissioned French submarine for public display. Clear views into the pens may be had from the opposite side of the basin.

Follow the same route as for Brest, but from the D69, turn on to the D764 at the junction with the N12 – signposted Quimper. Follow the D764 until its junction with the D18, and the D18 until its junction with the N165/E60. Follow this main route past Junction 17 and turn onto the D773 which is signposted St Nazaire. Follow this to its junction with the N171, and then follow the N171 for about 10km until reaching the N471, which leads into the city.

## La Pallice

The bunker at La Pallice is still owned by the French Navy but is not in military use: two of the original pens have been leased out for civilian use. Nature has achieved what the bombs of the RAF and USAAF failed to do: the bunker, lacking the requisite maintenance, is now in poor condition and considered too dangerous to be kept in use. The bunker lies close to the quay from which the ferries run to the Isle de Ré, and an excellent view into the pens can be had from the long jetty which runs out between pens 7 and 8. Access to this jetty is not restricted. Access to the rear and sides of the bunker complex is also possible. The bunker was used for location shots for the film *Das Boot*, which also provides fine views both internal and external of this site.

Follow the same route as for Bordeaux as far as Junction 7 on the A83/E3. Here, turn on to the N137 and follow this to the junction with the N11 some 43km further on. Here, turn on to the N11/E601. La Rochelle/La Pallice is only 10km from here.

# Further reading and research

The following titles may be of particular interest to the reader:

Angolia, John R and Littlejohn, David *Labor Organisations of the Reich*, R James Bender Publishing, San Jose, 1999

Fröhle, Claude and Kühn, Hans-Jürgen *Hochseefestung Helgoland*, Fröhle-Kühn Verlagsgesellschaft, Herbolzheim, 1999

Neitzel, Sönke *Die deutschen Ubootbunker und Bunkerwerften*, Bernard /Graefe Verlag, 1991

Rössler, Eberhard *The Type XXI U-Boat (Anatomy of the Ship)*, Naval Institute Press, 2002

Schmeelke, Karl-Heinz and Michael *German U-Boat Bunkers – Yesterday and Today*, Schiffer Publishing, Altglen, 1999

Schmidt, Dieter and Becker, Fabian *Bunker Valentin*, Edition Temmen, Bremen, Rostock, 1996

Showell, Jak P Mallmann *German Navy Handbook*, Sutton Publishing, 1999

*After the Battle* magazine (Battle of Britain Prints, London). No. 55 (1995) contains excellent information and photos of the U-Boat bases in France. No. 111 (2001) contains an in-depth feature on the demolition of the Hamburg U-Boat bunkers.

There are also a number of excellent on-line reference resources where additional information and photographs may be viewed. The best of these is certainly **http://www.uboatnet** which contains a huge volume of information about every possible aspect of the U-Boats during World War II and includes information on the U-Boat bunkers. The site **http://www.uboatbases.com** provides excellent data on the French U-Boat bases, and a further site at **http://perso.club-internat.fr/barbara9** provides information specifically on the La Pallice bunker.

The finest single repository of data of any type on the U-Boats of both world wars is without doubt the **U-Boot Archiv** in Cuxhaven. Under the guiding hand of its director, Horst Bredow, himself a U-Boat veteran, this has become the world's foremost source of U-Boat information.

The Archiv is located in a large detached villa and as well as containing a sizeable museum collection of original U-Boat artefacts, it has a massive photographic and documentary collection, much of which was donated from the photo albums of surviving U-Boat crewmen: this includes a large amount of material on the various U-Boat bunkers and bases.

The facilities of the Archiv are available to those who wish to visit in person, but prior arrangements must be made. The Archiv is a registered charity. No fee is charged for entry, and the Archiv depends on its visitors making a suitable donation after their visit. The Archiv will also, on payment of a suitable fee, carry out research on behalf of those who cannot visit.

For further details, contact Horst Bredow, U-Boot Archiv, Altenbrucher-Bahnhfstrasse, Cuxhaven, Germany, enclosing two International Reply Coupons.

There also exists an association known as the Circle of Friends of the U-Boat Archive (*Freundeskreis Traditionsarchiv U-Boote*) which publishes a regular newsletter often featuring fascinating information unearthed from the Archiv's collection of original documents.

For further information, contact the Archiv: alternatively, English-speaking enthusiasts may contact Jak P Mallmann-Showell, 2 Lookers Lane, Saltwood, Hythe, Kent, UK, again enclosing two International Reply Coupons.

ABOVE The rear of the St Nazaire bunker today. The stains of nearly 60 years' exposure to the elements are the only signs of deterioration on this imposing edifice. (Chris Boonzaier)

RIGHT Many of the subsidiary, smaller bunkers dotted around the U-Boat bases (used for the safe storage of torpedoes and munitions away from the main complex) are still intact and used as storage facilities. (Chris Boonzaier)

# Glossary

**Accumulatorraum** Battery store
**Bassin** Basin
**Beton** Concrete
**Büro** Office
**Caisson** Cofferdam
**Deck** Ceiling, roof
**Deckenträger** Roof support
**Dreherei** Turning shop (lathe workshop)
**Electro-Werke** Generator room
**Fangrost** System of interlacing concrete beams above
  a bunker's roof to create a protective layer and
  prevent bomb damage
**Flakstand** Anti-aircraft station, gun position
**Heizwerk** Heating works
**Hafen** Harbour
**Innenhafen** Inner harbour
**Kai** Quay
**Kesselhaus** Boiler house
**Kran** Crane
**Lager** Store
**Luftschutzbunker** Air raid shelter
**Magazin** Magazine
**Nassbock** A 'wet' pen
**Panzertore** Armoured door
**Ponton** Pontoon
**Pumpenraum** Pump room
**Rammpfähle** Pile-driver
**Sehrohr Werkstatt** Periscope workshop
**Schiffs-Reparaturwerk** Ship repair works
**Sauerstoffanlage** Oxygen plant
**Schleusse** Lock
**Sperrballon** Barrage balloon
**Tischlerei** Carpenters' workshop
**Torpedolager** Torpedo store
**Trockenbock** A dry-dock-capable pen
**Werkstatt** Workshop

# Index